the *Call* to

JOY
&
PAIN

Embracing Suffering in Your Ministry

the Call to

JOY

&

PAIN

Ajith Fernando

CROSSWAY BOOKS
WHEATON, ILLINOIS

The Call to Joy and Pain

Copyright © 2007 by Ajith Fernando

Published in association with the literary agency of Wolgemuth and Associates

Published by Crossway Books
    a publishing ministry of Good News Publishers
    1300 Crescent Street
    Wheaton, Illinois 60187

Cover design: Jon McGrath

Cover photo: iStock

First printing, 2007

Printed in the United States of America

Unless otherwise indicated, Scripture quotations are taken from *The Holy Bible: English Standard Version®*. Copyright © 2001 by Crossway Bibles, a publishing ministry of Good News Publishers. Used by permission. All rights reserved.

References cited as from NIV are from *The Holy Bible, New International Version*. Copyright © 1973, 1978, 1984 by International Bible Society. Used by permission of Zondervan Publishing House. All rights reserved. The "NIV" and "New International Version" trademarks are registered in the United States Patent and Trademark Office by International Bible Society. Use of either trademark requires the permission of International Bible Society.

References cited as from NASB are from *New American Standard Bible*. Copyright © 1960, 1962, 1963, 1968, 1971, 1972, 1973, 1975, 1977, 1995 by The Lockman Foundation and are used by permission.

References cited as from ASV are from *Holy Bible: American Standard Version*.

References cited as from KJV are from *The Holy Bible: King James Version*.

Library of Congress Cataloging-in-Publication Data
Fernando, Ajith.
  The call to joy and pain : embracing suffering in your ministry /
Ajith Fernando.
    p. cm.
  ISBN 978-1-58134-888-0 (tpb)
  1. Suffering—Religious aspects—Christianity. I. Title.
BV4909.F47   2007
348.8'6—dc22   2007006474

VP		17	16	15	14	13	12	11	10	09	08	07
15	14	13	12	11	10	9	8	7	6	5	4	3	2	1

To

DOREEN WIRASINHA

SUMANTH and MANEL WIRASINHA

ROY and DILKUSH PERERA

And to the memory of

RONALD WIRASINHA

Because of them, *in-laws* is a term that brings great joy,
reminding me of some of God's choicest blessings

CONTENTS

Part Four
SERVANTS OF THE CHURCH

A CONCLUDING MEDITATION

INTRODUCTION

Now I rejoice in my sufferings for your sake, and in my flesh I am filling up what is lacking in Christ's afflictions for the sake of his body, that is, the church, of which I became a minister according to the stewardship from God that was given to me for you, to make the word of God fully known, the mystery hidden for ages and generations but now revealed to his saints. To them God chose to make known how great among the Gentiles are the riches of the glory of this mystery, which is Christ in you, the hope of glory. Him we proclaim, warning everyone and teaching everyone with all wisdom, that we may present everyone mature in Christ. For this I toil, struggling with all his energy that he powerfully works within me.

COLOSSIANS 1:24-29

The Bible often describes suffering as an essential aspect of the Christian life. Therefore this should be a theme that appears often in Christian thinking and communication. Yet, with the affluence and technological advancement of the twenty-first century, many have come to regard comfort and convenience as essential human rights. Therefore the biblical message of the essentialness of the cross has become culturally incompatible with the way many think today. The need for more reflection on this issue has become especially acute because some popular Christian teachers say that it is not God's will for Christians to suffer. Some say that because Christ bore the curse for us, we should not bear this aspect of the curse—suffering—anymore. That would suggest that there is something seriously wrong in our lives if we suffer.

I have discussed the issue of suffering in most of my books, but I have felt—and many friends have suggested—that I should write an entire book on the topic. I was grateful for the opportunity to give some concentrated attention because of an invitation by John Piper to speak at the Bethlehem Pastors' Conference in January-February 2006 on "How Must a Pastor Die?" When Dr. Lane Dennis and Al Fisher of Crossway Books knew that I was going to give this series, they suggested I develop those talks into a book. As always, it is a joy to work with the folks at Crossway and to benefit again from the editorial expertise of Ted Griffin.

Since the Bethlehem Pastors' Conference I have spoken on the topic of this book in many places. The most moving experience for me was teaching a group of pastors in Cambodia under the "Timothy's All" program. Many of them had suffered immensely during the "Killing Fields" years under the Khmer Rouge. It seemed that this material helped them process their experience using biblical categories. The discussion times on that occasion were so intense that we had to reschedule the sessions—one speaker even graciously gave up his session to allow for more time. Strangely, even in Cambodia the teaching that Christians should not suffer at all seems to be growing.

One of the early decisions I made during my preparation for the Bethlehem Conference was to follow the biblical practice of not talking about pain without also talking about the blessings of it. Joy is a commonly mentioned blessing of suffering in the New Testament. The passage that I took as a base from which to work—Colossians 1:24-29—presents joy and pain together. So the decision was made to study both joy and pain. We will show in this book that something is seriously wrong not when Christians suffer but when they do not have the joy of the Lord.

The Bible knows nothing of the dour calls to the duty of suffering that many associate with the cross. The overwhelming attitude of the Bible regarding pain and suffering in the life of the Christian is positive. Even in the book of Revelation the reality of persecution and martyrdom is constantly colored by the thought of the heavenly reward for the faithful and punishment for the wicked.

My hope is that this book will help Christians look at suffering as something to be embraced because the sovereign Lord has seen fit to have them endure it. We should not go after suffering, but when it comes, we can look at it through the eyes of faith. Without such an approach to suffering, it will not be possible for us to experience the joy that the Bible describes as an essential aspect of the Christian life. The great American missionary to India E. Stanley Jones describes this attitude well when he says, "Don't bear trouble, use it. Take whatever happens—justice and injustice, pleasure and pain, compliment and criticism—take it up into the purpose of your life and make something out of it. Turn it into testimony."[1]

Today in the church we have a lot of emphasis on a *therapy* for suffering but insufficient emphasis on a *theology* of suffering, which must form the basis of all therapy for suffering. Without an adequate theology regarding suffering, Christians avoid the cross and move away from their call, and they are also unnecessarily unhappy when they face pain. I trust that this book will help people look at suffering biblically and by so doing help them to be happy and obedient Christians. It does not deal with all the issues relating to a theology of suffering, especially the issue of why there is suffering in the world.[2] But it attempts to present a practical Christian theology of suffering. I have presented the material in the form of thirty short, biblical meditations so that the book could be used as a month's devotional guide.

On this our thirtieth anniversary year, I wish to express my special thanks to God for my wife, Nelun. Because of her love for God she has borne with all the trials that come with being married to a Christian worker with a call that sometimes makes life difficult for her and with weaknesses that clearly call for loads of Christian patience. I also thank her for reading through this manuscript and making many valuable suggestions.

Part One

SUFFERING AND JOY ARE BASIC TO CHRISTIANITY

Now I rejoice in my sufferings for your sake.

COLOSSIANS 1:24A

Chapter One

TWO BASIC ASPECTS OF CHRISTIANITY

After the death of his wife Paul Tournier, regarded as the father of contemporary Christian counseling, wrote a book titled *Creative Suffering*. There he shows how suffering can be a trigger for great creativity. He talks about the sorrow he experienced over the death of his father when he was two years old and that of his mother when he was five years old and then the death of his wife. He says, "The human heart does not obey the rules of logic: it is constitutionally contradictory. I can truly say that I have a great grief and that I am a happy man."[1]

Tournier's statement places before us the basic premise of this book. Pain and joy are both essential features of Christianity. Paul's statement at the start of the section we are using as the base for this book (Col. 1:24) makes the same affirmation: "Now I rejoice in my sufferings for your sake."

THE CALL TO JOY

Great Christians thinkers like C. S. Lewis and John Piper have emphasized that joy is perhaps the primary characteristic of a Christian. We may not realize it, but the Old Testament oozes with the theme of joy. There are twenty-three different Hebrew words for joy in the Old Testament. I read somewhere that Hebrew is the language that has the greatest number of words for joy. In two verses in Zephaniah alone (3:14, 17) seven different words for joy are found!

The Old Testament has several calls and commands to people to rejoice. I used my computer concordance to trace the use of the English word *rejoice* in calls to and decisions to rejoice and in reports of rejoicing by God and God's people. I found eighty-one references. The Psalms with thirty-one references, Isaiah with thirteen, and Deuteronomy with ten head the list. There are instruments in Old Testament worship, such as cymbals, that are particularly suited for expressing joy. Believers are urged to clap their hands for joy (Ps. 47:1). The Psalms speak of shouting for joy twelve times, and singing is mentioned eighty-seven times. We know that singing is most often an expression of joy. Singing and joy come together thirteen times in the Psalms. Then there is the succession of festivals in the Jewish calendar. Festivals are generally times dedicated to expressing joy. It is clear, then, that joy and the expression of it are important in the Old Testament.

The same is true of the New Testament. The first announcement of the birth of Christ by the angels was described as "good news of great joy that will be for all the people" (Luke 2:10). "And the shepherds returned, glorifying and praising God for all they had heard and seen" (Luke 2:20). Matthew is emphatic in his description of the response of the Wise Men to seeing the baby Jesus: "They rejoiced exceedingly with great joy" (Matt. 2:10).

With an even more marked experience of salvation in the New Testament than in the Old Testament, we can see that the joy of salvation has an important place in the Bible. We see this in the three parables of salvation in Luke 15 where the finding of the lost sheep, the lost coin, and the lost son are all accompanied by great rejoicing and celebration (Luke 15:6-7, 9-10, 20-24). To me the description of the father, an elderly, rich man wearing a long cloak, doing something quite unexpected in that day—running and publicly embracing and kissing his wayward child—is one of the most moving passages of the Bible. But it doesn't finish with that. The father gathered his friends together and celebrated with a party with music and dancing.

So the members of the first church in Jerusalem would meet in their homes and eat "with glad and generous [or sincere] hearts" (Acts 2:46). And when salvation came to a town in Samaria "there was much joy in that city" (Acts 8:8). Later Paul would place joy right after love in his listing of the fruit of the Spirit (Gal. 5:22). Writing from prison he instructed the Christians to rejoice and even repeated his instruction for emphasis: "Rejoice in the Lord always; again I will say, Rejoice" (Phil. 4:4). In a passage giving instructions in response to the controversy over dietary laws in the church, Paul, wanting to place the emphasis where it should be, said, "For the kingdom of God is not a matter of eating and drinking but of righteousness and peace and joy in the Holy Spirit" (Rom. 14:17).

Salvation is such an overwhelmingly wonderful blessing that whatever we go through, we always have a reason to rejoice. One of the great preachers of the early Methodist church was a miner from Cornwall, Billy Bray (1794–1868), who had been a drunkard and an immoral man before his conversion. He could never get over the joy of knowing that God had saved him and made him "the King's son." His life was one incessant act of joyous praise to God, and he felt the joy of salvation was so immense that it needed to be expressed. He said, "Well, I dance sometimes. Why shouldn't I dance as well as David? David, you say, was a king; well, bless the Lord! I am a King's son! I have as good a right to dance as David had. Bless the Lord! I get very happy at times; my soul gets full of the glory, and then I dance too!"[2]

Clearly to Billy Bray joy was a primary feature of Christianity. Working in the mines was a dangerous business, and there was always the possibility of dying in the mine. He would tell his fellow miners that they must pray before they go down. They would ask him to pray. He would pray, "Lord, if any of us must be killed, or die to-day, let it be *me*; let not one of these men die, for they are not happy; but I am, and if I die to-day I shall go to heaven." Bray said, "When I rose from my knees, I should see the tears running down their faces; and soon after some of them became praying men too."[3] It is easy to get so sophisticated about Christianity that we miss the joy of salvation that the Bible speaks about.

THE CALL TO SUFFER

We will spend a considerable amount of time in this book looking at the texts that present the call to pain and suffering. Let me simply affirm here that this too is a basic aspect of Christianity. Jesus' basic call to follow him was a call to suffer: "If anyone would come after me, let him deny himself and take up his cross and follow me" (Matt. 16:24). His hearers would have known that he was speaking of severe suffering when he said this because they knew that crucifixion was a cruel and painful way of causing death. Jesus told us, "In the world you will have tribulation" (John 16:33). And Paul stated, "Indeed, all who desire to live a godly life in Christ Jesus will be persecuted" (2 Tim. 3:12).

Jesus did not want people to follow him without realizing there was a cost involved in doing so. So he included the cost in his basic call to discipleship. When some would-be followers volunteered, he presented the cost to them in places where they were vulnerable (Luke 9:57-62). We are not told, but it is quite possible that they decided not to follow Jesus. We know for sure that the rich young ruler did not follow Christ because the cost Jesus presented was too great for him (Matt. 19:16-22). These two passages may be the sections where Christ's evangelistic methodology most radically differs from much of contemporary evangelism.

THEY COME TOGETHER

One of the interesting things about the New Testament record is that suffering is hardly ever mentioned without also a mention of the blessings of suffering. And often the blessing mentioned is joy. I was able to locate eighteen different places in the New Testament where suffering and joy are found together. The texts I found making this connection between suffering and joy were in the Gospels, the book of Acts, and the epistles. We also know that though Revelation may not mention this connection explicitly, it is implied there.

So according to the Bible, joy and pain can coexist. Christians don't talk about suffering unless they also talk about the joy of suffering. It is the joy that makes the cross worthwhile, for it gives us the strength to bear it. As Nehemiah said, "The joy of the LORD is your strength" (Neh. 8:10).

I once heard David Sitton, the founder of To Every Tribe Mission, tell how when he was a teenager a ninety-year-old missionary spoke at the youth fellowship of his church. He had been a missionary for seventy-two years. At the start of his talk he kept saying the same thing over and over again. It was something like, "I want you to remember this. You can forget everything I say, but don't forget this." He kept saying something like this for about five minutes, and the young people were getting impatient, wishing he would go ahead and say it. Finally he said what he wanted to say: "The joy of the Lord is your strength. When the joy goes, the strength goes." Having said that, he sat down!

That is the basic affirmation of this book. Joy and suffering are necessary aspects of Christianity. And they can and must exist together.

Chapter Two

A FORGOTTEN TREASURE

For years I had thought that one of the greatest attractions of Christianity was the joy that salvation brings. Now I have my doubts about that. I have come to realize that many people are willing to sacrifice joy in order to get some other things that they think are essential for their life.

SATISFACTION VERSUS JOY

It seems that people don't have a taste for joy and that they would rather have success in sports or in their career or in sexual conquest or through material prosperity or in taking revenge against someone who has hurt them.

In Sri Lanka the cultural push for revenge is one of the huge challenges we have when working with people who have come to Christ from other faiths. People are supposed to hit back if someone dishonors their family. If they don't, they are viewed as cowards or as having insulted the family honor. Often we see leaders pressing hard to show that they are right and the organization or church was wrong when it decided against their advice. We see Christians who have been insulted by another Christian work hard to expose the faults of the person who insulted them. These efforts may take away their joy and inflame anger in their hearts. But they cannot resist the temptation to work to have the satisfaction of hitting back.

Perhaps the most extreme form of this quest for satisfaction at the cost of joy is addiction. Even though individuals know that drugs or pornography or gambling will take away their joy and the joy of those who love them, they still cannot go without that habit. They sacrifice so much for a shallow kick. And the satisfaction of getting this thing that they want is even more important to them than their happiness.

I think one reason for this is that people do not know what a wonderful thing joy is. Not having tasted the fullness of joy, they are too easily satisfied with the fake satisfaction that these other activities bring. In our pleasure-crazy culture the call of the psalmist is certainly relevant: "Oh, taste and see that the LORD is good! Blessed is the man who takes refuge in him!" (Ps. 34:8).

WHAT IS THE JOY OF THE LORD?

We can describe the joy that the gospel brings as "the joy of the LORD" (Neh. 8:10) or as rejoicing in the Lord (Phil. 4:4). This joy has as its base some great truths that undergird our lives.

- We believe in God.
- We believe that he loves us and that in love he gave us his Son to die for us.
- We believe that he has made us his children and looks after us and that he's for us so that no one can stand against us.
- He lives in us, banishing loneliness.
- He turns the bad things that happen to us into good things.
- He loves us more than the unkindness that we experience in life, and he is able to comfort and to heal us when we are wounded.

• He has prepared an inheritance that we will receive after this life that is more wonderful than anything we could ever imagine.

These wonderful truths and many, many others are the basis upon which we have built our lives. They open the way for a love relationship with God. While the relationship is essentially an experiential love relationship, the basis of our relationship is this list of objective, unchanging truths. We can cling to them when everything about us seems gloomy.

Love is the happiest word in our vocabulary. I was out of town on my last birthday and came home during the night. When I went to my room, there was a large card on my table. I usually compose my own birthday cards for my family members. My wife usually buys cards, but she goes to great pains to ensure that she purchases one with appropriate words. And the words in this one beautifully described our relationship. I was so thrilled! I sat basking in the fact that after thirty years together my wife still loved me. Suddenly it dawned upon me that God's love is so much greater. If a wife's love brings that much joy, how much more joy does God's love. David described it like this: "You make known to me the path of life; in your presence there is fullness of joy; at your right hand are pleasures forevermore" (Ps. 16:11). To be sure, the experience David described is not our constant feeling. But this experience arises out of a deep and unchanging reality that undergirds our lives—namely, the almighty God loves us and looks after us. So we can say with Habakkuk:

> *Though the fig tree should not blossom, nor fruit be on the vines, the produce of the olive fail and the fields yield no food, the flock be cut off from the fold and there be no herd in the stalls, yet I will rejoice in the LORD; I will take joy in the God of my salvation.*
> HAB. 3:17-18

My closest friend died of cancer in 2005. The last time he went to the hospital he was in great pain. He was gradually slipping into a semiconscious state. One of the last things he told me was that someone once said, "I have hit rock bottom, and I find that the

Rock is solid!" Deuteronomy 33:27 says, "The Eternal God is your dwelling place, and underneath are the everlasting arms."

Even as we go through disappointments, pain, and stress, we know that God is with us and that he has promised to turn these tough experiences into something good. That gives us great relief amidst the pain.

Early in our marriage my wife and I agreed that we will not go to sleep if there is tension between us. In the early years we would have some interesting "love-fights"[1] that would drag into the night. But when the resolution came, it was sweet. I might go to work the next morning with red eyes because of lack of sleep but with the freedom of knowing that things were right with the one I love. During those arguments I got into the habit of praying with my heart while talking to my wife with my mouth. And usually the prayer went something like, "Please, God—please, God—please, God—help."

What a relief it was to know that God was right there when we were going through the crisis. That banishes fear and enables us to hope for a resolution and prevents us from acting rashly. We may be weeping inside, we may be hurting from the bruises we have received, but deep down we know that God is with us and that he is our source of joy. The happiest people in the world are not those who don't have problems—they are those who are not afraid of problems.

REAL LIBERATION

What deliverance God brings. We are freed from bondage to fear. We have something more reliable than fickle experiences. Our life is founded on unchanging truths that open us to a love relationship with an unchanging God. No wonder Jesus said, "You will know the truth, and the truth will set you free" (John 8:32). He went on to say, "If the Son sets you free, you will be free indeed" (John 8:36).

Postmodern people say they want to be freed from the tyranny of objective truth that, they say, has deprived humans of authentic experience. They want to focus more on the subjective experiences into which their instincts take them. We do not deny the priority of experience. In fact, we say that experience is basic to Christianity. If we have given people the idea that Christianity is based wholly on a bunch of propositions, we have given them a wrong idea. Christianity *is* based on propositions that are found in the Bible. But these propositions open the door to authentic experiences that enable us to truly embrace our humanity.

The experience we have is not a boringly predictable thing that, again, our critics would say is evidence that we are not truly free. The different ways people come to Christ and the varied experiences they have would convince us that there is nothing boringly predictable about Christianity. For example, the Bible says that in our experience of receiving the gifts of the Spirit, God gives each Christian a unique gift. Paul uses two strong words—"apportions" (1 Cor. 12:11) and "measure" (Eph. 4:7)—to say that God gives a combination of gifts specifically designed for each member. There's a niche for each Christian. Of course, those who do not submit to God's lordship would say they want to be free to choose the experiences they are going to have. We, however, say that true freedom is when the God who made us gives us what is best for us.

One neglected aspect of biblical religion that evangelicals have embraced because of the postmodern emphasis on experience is that sometimes God sends us an experience that opens the door to accepting a proposition. Peter, for example, accepted the important proposition about the breaking of barriers in Christ between Jews and Gentiles after experiencing a vision. This sequence of experience leading to accepting a proposition has taken place with several liberal Christian scholars who changed their theological orientation to a more biblical or evangelical persuasion after they had a charismatic experience or saw God perform a miracle. A once strongly liberal New Testament scholar, Etta Linnemann, who was a professor in Germany and an esteemed student of the famous scholar Rudolf Bultmann, is an example of this. She has written a book in which she explains her journey from skepticism to belief in the authority of Scripture.[2] But even here, though one comes to accept the truth via experience, the biblical propositions accepted are basic.

These experiences of Christians are uncertain things that cannot be relied on because they depend on circumstances. The reality that lies behind these experiences does not change with the change of circumstances. Our experience is based on unchanging truths that lead to a love relationship with an unchanging God.

What good news this is in a world characterized by so much uncertainty. C. S. Lewis has a beautiful section on the question of why the psalmists delighted in the Law in his book *Reflections on the Psalms*. The English Standard Version has the psalmists saying that they delight in God's Law or Word twelve times. Lewis says it is a mystery to him that people can rejoice in this way in the Law.[3] One can imagine people fearing the Law or respecting the Law. But how can they delight in it? After delving into possible reasons for this, Lewis concludes, "Their delight in the law is a delight in having touched firmness; like the pedestrian delights in feeling the hard road beneath his feet after a false shortcut has long entangled him in muddy fields."[4]

I sensed this once when I was hiking with some friends in the mountains. We decided to take a shortcut and got lost. On the way we saw droppings of wild boar, which frightened us. But we went in what we thought was the direction of the town. Then we came to a real road. What a relief and joy that was!

With such security, with such confidence, we are freed to enjoy life to the fullest. We know that even problems are turned into something good, that they are gateways to joy. The world doesn't know such joy; so it has settled for a shallow kick called pleasure or satisfaction. But this is not real satisfaction or pleasure. C. S. Lewis says, "Joy is not a substitute for sex; sex is very often a substitute for Joy. I sometimes wonder whether all pleasures are not substitutes for Joy."[5] The problem with us is that we are too easily satisfied.

What we have argued for here is that the joy of the Lord is deeper, more reliable, and more fulfilling than the various pleasures people are looking for without God.

Chapter Three

BURSTS OF PLEASURE

An important aspect of the rhythm of human experience is what we can call bursts of pleasure. Different people experience this in different ways. Some have parties on the weekends that they look forward to all week. At special times, such as after an exam or when the school term closes, young people resort to binge drinking and consume huge amounts of alcohol. Some find pleasure through sports or hobbies, whether by watching or participating. Various kinds of sexual experiences provide this for others. Some of these bursts of pleasure are good for us, such as sexual relations with one's spouse or music or sports. Others are harmful.

The Bible also has a place for these bursts of pleasure. In the Christian life there is a rhythm of life in which moments of ecstasy or increased pleasure are an important bonus to the daily discipline of ordinary living. God made us with the capacity for ecstasy and expects us to use it.

In the life of a married person, that ecstasy can come from sexual relations. It is a mountaintop experience that gives expression to the physical, mental, and spiritual union that is part of the daily life of the couple. The Old Testament prescribed regular festivals for the Jewish people, and in some of them a major part of the agenda was celebration. The celebration was about God's provision, a fact that was true every day of their life. Those festivals celebrated that in a special way, but that is not something we can do with intensity every day. Sexual relations between spouses and festivals don't create joy; they give expression to a joy that is already there. Christian ecstasy is a supplement to joy, not a substitute for joy.

India had a great Christian evangelist named Sadhu Sundar Singh (1889–c.1929). He was from a devout Sikh family, and as a young man he would go into the mountains and meditate using Hindu and Sikh disciplines. "He attained a mastery of the Yoga technique and became oblivious to the external world for short spells. During those moments he experienced in some measure the peace and joy for which his soul craved. But when he returned to consciousness, he was again plunged into the turmoil of unrest and discontent."[1] He opposed Christianity vehemently, even trampling Bibles and throwing mud at the homes of missionaries. But he was in a desperate search for *shanthi* or peace.

Not finding *shanthi*, Sundar Singh decided to commit suicide by standing in front of an early-morning express train that passed his house. Just before he went to the tracks he had a vision of Christ and was converted. And he not only became a great evangelist—he became a master of the Christian disciplines. Now he found the *shanthi* he had searched for in non-Christian spiritual disciplines. He did not give up having ecstatic experiences. But now such experiences had to do with the God who came back to the valley with him when he came down from his mountaintop experience. Sundar Singh once said, "Without Christ I am like a fish out of water; with Christ I am in an ocean of love." That's what Christ does to us. He not only gives us ecstatic experiences, he also remains with us and gives us peace and joy all through life. He fulfills the deep yearnings of our hearts.

I work for Youth for Christ, and we are committed to give youth times of great fun. I often say that we are serious about fun in Youth for Christ. And that comes out of a theology of pleasure. The God who created our capacity for fun is the one who can give us the most satisfying experience of pleasure. So hilarious enjoyment can be considered a religious activity that is done in companionship with God.

I think the best example of a shallow kick that does not truly satisfy is the way many people have sexual pleasure. In Christianity, sex is the summit of physical, emotional, and spiritual oneness. It gets deeper and more enjoyable with time because of that. Today sex has become a biological necessity to many people. They look at it as a physical need that must be met, whether they are married or not. Some people say that the purest and most sublime form of sex is when two people who do not know each other come together in a purely physical act and then move away. They do not even care to know each other's names. But we are made for committed love, and it is in such love that deep fulfillment is found. Recent studies have demonstrated that married couples enjoy sex more than cohabiting couples.[2] Sex is supposed to be accompanied by lifelong commitment to each other. Without that, sex has a hollow ring to it. Without the joy of the Lord, *all* pleasure has a hollow ring to it. It leaves you a short time after the experience is over.

Let me say that we need to develop a rhythm that includes bursts of pleasure to punctuate our daily experience of joy. Families need to bring this into their routines. Parents must make sure that the home is a happy, affirming, and peaceful place for their children to grow up in. And they need to ensure that there are frequent special fun times such as games, vacations, special meals, and celebrations.

Yet while joy is an absolutely essential thing for a fulfilled life, these bursts of pleasure can be missed if circumstances require that. Sickness may make sexual relations impossible. Single people will not have this at all. The need to visit a friend who is sick may make you miss a game that you hoped to watch. Yet even without these,

Christians can be fulfilled individuals because the basic source of fulfillment lies elsewhere. If we don't have joy as a part of everyday life, we will depend too much on a burst of pleasure for fulfillment, and if that fails us we will be unhappy. Even vacations can be stressful times for families. Families look forward to them with so much anticipation that when something goes wrong, they may become disappointed and despondent.

So today we need to show people what a wonderful thing joy is. We need to show how joyful joy is, that the freedom that comes from submission to permanent committed relationships with God and with a spouse is an incomparable experience. We need to show that we too have bursts of true pleasure. Then people, in their mad quest for pleasure in this hedonistic age, will realize that what they are searching for is found only in the way of life ordained by their Creator.

Chapter Four

LAMENT

Having looked at how joy and pain coexist in the Christian life, it is time to present three things that are usually needed before we experience joy in the midst of pain. The first of these is not absolutely essential all the time, but the other two are. The first is lament. Christians need not deny pain. At some time all Christians experience pain, discouragement, sorrow, and anger over wrong things and misfortunes that affect them. It is not helpful to deny these feelings. Often before we rejoice amidst pain we need to mourn or lament or express our pain in some such way.

In theology there is an expression, *now and not yet*, which describes the present age in which we live. The Old Testament looked forward to the age to come. With the coming of Christ this age dawned. However, the end is not yet. The work of Christ will be consummated when he comes again. Until then we experience the features of the new age in what can be called a foretaste. There are still features of the old age.

This theology is well explained in Romans 8:19-25. Paul says that because of the fall, "the creation was subjected to futility [or frustration, NIV] . . . in hope" by God. The result of this is that we get sick and find our abilities diminishing with age, and we eventually die. People fail us or harm us, and we often get hurt. We await the day when "the creation itself will be set free from its bondage to corruption and obtain the freedom of the glory of the children of God" (v. 21). Until then we have "the firstfruits of the spirit" (v. 23), giving us a foretaste of the glory that awaits us at the consummation. During this waiting period, Paul says, "the whole creation has been groaning together in the pains of childbirth until now" (v. 22). Even believers join in this groaning: "And not only the creation, but we ourselves, who have the firstfruits of the Spirit, groan inwardly as we wait eagerly for adoption as sons, the redemption of our bodies" (v. 23).

This groaning finds expression in the Old Testament in what is called the lament. Scholars classify fifty to sixty of the 150 Psalms as laments—that is a little over a third of the Psalms. A whole book of the Bible, Lamentations, is a series of laments over the destruction of Jerusalem. In fact "every prophetic book except Haggai includes one or more examples of the lament genre."[1] Clinton McCann points out that though lament psalms far outnumber psalms of praise in the book of Psalms, songs of praise outnumber songs of lament sixteen to six in the Presbyterian hymnal.[2] I think the gap is wider in most contemporary hymnals.

The laments are cries of the righteous who despite their faithfulness are going through great hardship. Old Testament scholar Chris Wright describes the content of a biblical lament like this: "God, I am hurting; and God, everyone else is laughing. And God, You are not helping very much either; and how long is it going to go on?"[3] So we mourn, we weep, we groan because of the pain, we ask why this problem happened to us, and we grapple with the theological questions we have over what happened.

This idea of lament is somewhat strange in some cultures, especially for men. In the Bible we find both men and women lamenting. Even Jesus lamented over Jerusalem (Luke 13:34-35) and later wept over it (Luke 19:41). And we know how he wept when he went to the tomb of Lazarus (John 11:35). Speaking to his disciples about his coming death and resurrection, he said, "Truly, truly, I say to you, you will weep and lament, but the world will rejoice. You will be sorrowful, but your sorrow will turn into joy" (John 16:20).

As I tried to think biblically about how Christians should respond to the tsunami that hit Sri Lanka in 2004, I realized that we were not in the habit of lamenting as the people in Bible times did when there was a national disaster. I preached at my home church two weeks after the tsunami, and we introduced a ritual of lament, mourning over what had happened and identifying with our suffering people and pleading for God to bring relief to our people. If corporate laments are not part of our community life, it would be good to restore the practice in the church. And certainly we need to learn how we can give suitable expression to our pain when we are personally hurt.

We must remember that with personal laments we usually lament to God and to his people. When we do that we open ourselves to God's comfort, which he directly gives to us or which he mediates through his people. Paul describes God as "the . . . God of all comfort, who comforts us in all our affliction" (2 Cor. 1:3b-4a). He delights to minister to us, and his comfort deepens the most precious thing in our lives—our love relationship with him.

Once when we were having some serious problems in our ministry, I came home after a meeting deeply hurt. I lay in bed and burst into tears. My son walked into the room and for the first time saw his father crying. He went to his mother and asked what was wrong. She told him that I was having serious problems at work. Then he went to my computer, opened my e-mail address book, and wrote a letter to some of my best friends. It said that I was going through a lot of stress and asked for prayer for me. When I heard that he had done this, I was thrilled. I think the pain of that difficult time is leaving me, but I think I will always remember and be impacted by the kindness shown by my son.

By opening ourselves to God's comfort we also open ourselves to healing from bitterness. We are bitter when we think of an event in purely negative terms. If God has comforted us, even though the memory of the event is still painful, the bitterness will be gone because we have experienced a love that is greater than the harm done to us.

Having experienced God's comfort we are also able to face people, even people who have hurt us, with God's grace, which is greater than all sin. So we can be a constructive presence in unpleasant and angry situations. Our bitterness is gone. Now our full energies are given to finding a resolution rather than showing that we are right or teaching the person who hurt us a lesson.

Because of the war that we have had, ministry in Sri Lanka can be quite frustrating. We work hard at planning an event and find that a curfew is announced just before the event is held. We are often not able to do our usual ministries. I have found that sometimes it is the tough leaders who find this the most difficult to handle. In their toughness they haven't learned to lament and express their pain and frustration. Sometimes this frustration becomes so difficult to bear that they leave the country, saying they cannot do the work they are called to do because of the prevailing situation. Actually their tough exterior may be an expression of weakness. They are unable to make themselves vulnerable to feelings of frustration and pain. So they leave the situation.

The reader will recognize that what we have looked at here directly contradicts the teaching of those who say that because Jesus bore the curse on our behalf, we do not need to suffer like he did. In such teaching there is no place for lament. Lament would be an expression of distrust in God.

Brother Andrew has ministered in and for nations where Christians are persecuted for several decades. When he came to Sri Lanka I was at a meeting where he spoke. After his message there was a question time, and someone asked him what he thought about the type of prosperity theology that only talks of the blessings God gives without acknowledging pain and suffering. His answer was that you cannot proclaim such a theology in countries where Christians are persecuted. He said that if you want to hold such theology you will have to leave those countries, which is what some have done!

Chapter Five

FAITH AND ENDURANCE

The second necessity for joy amidst pain—faith—is always absolutely essential (unlike the earlier one, lament). In a well-known
joy/pain passage James says, "Count it all joy, my brothers, when
you meet trials of various kinds, for you know that the testing of
your faith produces steadfastness" (Jas. 1:2-3). We are to "count"
or "consider" (NIV) all our trials to be joyful. Because we believe
that a trial is going to work out for our good, we regard it as something we can respond to with joy.

Sadly, some Christians find this difficult to do. They have been
deeply hurt by people and circumstances. They did not see people
being committed to them when they needed it most because it was
too costly for them to do so. These painful experiences have affected
the way they look at life. And they find it difficult to believe that
the problems they face will work out for good. They even find it
difficult to believe that God will look after them in a difficult situa-

tion. So when problems come, they are not joyful. They think, *See, nothing works out right for me.*

One of the biggest challenges facing Christian workers is to help the people they care for to believe that God will look after them when they encounter trials. In fact, many Christian workers themselves need to be convinced of this. They simply can't accept that God delights to bless them. I counted seven verses in the Bible that state that God delights or takes pleasure in us,[1] three that say God delights in loving or blessing us,[2] and one that tells us that God delights in our welfare.[3] These eleven references state that we bring delight to God. Yet people who have faced rejection all their lives—whose parents or teachers or neighbors have pumped into their minds the message that they are useless—find this truth difficult to accept. They need to be convinced that they are capable of being loved and delighted in by God.

Sometimes before they can believe that God works for their good, they need to experience God's healing balm for the wounds that have caused them to look at life in a negative way. I have found that some people are open to this healing and find release as they forgive those who have hurt them and accept the truth that the sovereign God will use even the wounds they have received for their good. Others refuse to stop clinging to the idea that life has been bad to them. When they encounter any painful experience, they send that through the grid of their negative approach to life and end up bitter and angry. They regard the situation as another instance of things working out for bad rather than for good.

The belief that God works for our good usually grows as we have experiences that validate this scriptural truth. After several such validations, we learn to submit to what the Scriptures say about our painful experiences. And we affirm that even these will be used by God to become blessings to us. We learn to believe what the Bible says about pain in the life of a Christian.

Paul said, "And we know that for those who love God all things work together for good, for those who are called according to his purpose" (Rom. 8:28). Paul's affirmation of his belief, "we know," is in the perfect tense in the Greek. This tense is used for completed actions in the past, the effects of which are ongoing. When Paul said, "Christ has been raised from the dead" (1 Cor. 15:20), he used the perfect tense also. Even though the resurrection took place some time back, our Savior and Lord is still in a state of being risen. Paul uses the perfect tense five times in 1 Corinthians 15 to refer to the resurrection of Christ (vv. 13-14, 16-17, 20).

By using the perfect tense when he said, "we know that . . . all things work together for good," Paul seems to be implying that this conviction had come to him in the past and was still with him. The perfect tense is also used in Paul's famous statement of assurance that trials cannot separate us from the love of God: "For I am sure that neither death nor life, nor angels nor rulers, nor things present nor things to come, nor powers, nor height nor depth, nor anything else in all creation, will be able to separate us from the love of God in Christ Jesus our Lord" (Rom. 8:38-39).

When something terrible happens to Christians, they may weep and groan; they may get angry at the injustice of it all and even argue with God. But deep down in their hearts there is a truth that finally influences the way they respond to the problem—the truth that God will turn even this terrible thing into something good. They reason, "I have read it in God's Word. I have experienced it in my life. Now I know for sure that it will be OK."

Bernard Gilpin (1517–1583) was a preacher who was taken into custody for preaching the gospel during the time when Queen Mary was persecuting Protestants. He was being taken to London to certain death, but to the amusement of the guards accompanying him he kept saying, "Everything is for the best." On the way he fell off his horse and was hurt, so they could not travel for a few days. He told the amused guards, "I have no doubt but that even this painful accident will prove to be a blessing." Finally he was able to resume his journey. As they were nearing London later than expected, they heard the church bells ringing. They asked someone why this was so. They were told, "Queen Mary is dead, and there will be no more burning of Protestants." Gilpin looked at the guards and said, "Ah, you see, it is all for the best."[4] God used the delay caused by his painful fall to save his life.

The Bible often refers to endurance or patience in the midst of trials. Paul says, "We rejoice in our sufferings, knowing that suffering produces endurance" (Rom. 5:3). For such endurance we need faith and hope. Paul speaks of "endurance inspired by hope in our Lord Jesus Christ" (1 Thess. 1:3, NIV). He says, "But if we hope for what we do not see, we wait for it with patience" (Rom. 8:25). The above three references use the Greek word *hupomonē*, which is generally used for patience in the midst of trials. This is different from the word usually used for patience with individuals (*makrothumia*), often translated "long-suffering" in the older English versions.

The word *hupomonē*, used for endurance amidst trials, appears thirty-one times in the New Testament.[5] It means something different than what usually comes to our minds when we think of endurance. Usually we think of people stoically enduring hardship or accepting their unfortunate circumstances with passive resignation. But Christian patience is an *active* quality. It has more the idea of positive endurance than of passive resignation. Leon Morris explains, "It is the attitude of the soldier who in the thick of the battle is not dismayed but fights on stoutly whatever the difficulties."[6]

The great British Methodist preacher W. E. Sangster is a good example of Christian endurance. He was told he was dying of progressive muscular atrophy when he was in his prime as a preacher. His voice was one of the first things that he lost. He made four resolutions when he found out how serious his sickness was. They were: "(1) I will never complain; (2) I will keep the home bright; (3) I will count my blessings; (4) I will try to turn it to gain."[7] He kept himself busy until he died. His last book was written with two fingers and was sent to the publisher one or two days before he died.[8] Such endurance comes as a result of faith.

When our faith grows weak, we learn to preach to ourselves so that God's Word, which is the basis of our faith, may impact us. We see this in Psalm 42–43, which is actually one unit. It starts with the familiar words, "As a deer pants for flowing streams, so pants my soul for you, O God." Many who sing these words don't realize that they were written by a person who was in the depths of despair and to whom God seemed to be far away. In these two Psalms we find a refrain, which is actually a case of the psalmist preaching the same message to himself three times: "Why are you cast down, O my soul, and why are you in turmoil within me? Hope in God; for I shall again praise him, my salvation and my God" (42:5-6a; 42:11; 43:5).

Because our heart is struggling with the situation, our mind preaches to the heart the truths we know from the Word. In his classic book *Spiritual Depression* Dr. Martyn Lloyd-Jones asks, "Have you not realized that most of your unhappiness in life is due to the fact that you are listening to yourself instead of talking to yourself?"[9] We must learn to stop listening to our self-pitying conversation and start preaching the deeper realities to ourselves.

This function of feeding our faith by reminding us of deeper truths amidst dark experiences is most effectively performed through reading the Bible. David said, "If your law had not been my delight, I would have perished in my affliction" (Ps. 119:92). Martin Niemoller was a courageous German pastor who spent several years in prison because he spoke out against the unhealthy influence that Adolf Hitler's regime was having on the church in Germany. Speaking about the Bible he said, "What did this book mean to me during the long and weary years of solitary confinement and then for the last four years at Dachau [concentration camp]? The Word of God was simply everything to me—comfort and strength, guidance and hope, master of my days and companion of my nights, the bread which kept me from starvation and the water of life that refreshed my soul."[10]

The Christian who walks by faith, hoping in God in the midst of trouble, is described well in Paul's wish for the Romans: "May the God of hope fill you with all joy and peace in believing, so that by the power of the Holy Spirit you may abound in hope" (Rom. 15:13).

Chapter Six

SURRENDER

Just as faith is indispensable if we are to maintain joy in daily life, so is surrender. If we cling to anything in life, even a good thing, that thing will surely take away our joy. It may be a house that we have acquired. We can get so protective of it and so engrossed in making it the best house possible that we will lose our joy over that house. Any problem—and problems do come in these areas, especially if there are little children in the home—can take away our joy and make us act in ways that dishonor Christ.

I sometimes wonder whether the children of some homes are deprived of the merriment and spontaneous fun that are such an important part of a healthy childhood because their parents are so intent on keeping their house perfectly beautiful! To these children, home is not a fun place. That could give rise to a dangerous attitude, for when the children get older they may begin to think they can have real fun only outside the home. That often leads to sinful enjoyment with friends.

43

Because God knows our tendency to cling to things in an unhealthy way, he often calls us to surrender some of these idols so we can be freed from their hold on us. The New Testament presents this principle in different ways. Consider the following texts:

- If anyone would come after me, let him deny himself and take up his cross daily and follow me. For whoever would save his life will lose it, but whoever loses his life for my sake will save it. (Luke 9:23-24)
- I appeal to you therefore, brothers, by the mercies of God, to present your bodies as a living sacrifice, holy and acceptable to God, which is your spiritual worship. (Rom. 12:1)
- I die every day! (1 Cor. 15:31)
- I have been crucified with Christ. It is no longer I who live, but Christ who lives in me. (Gal. 2:20a)

Each of these texts implies that Christians constantly give up things that they like to keep in order to experience the freedom God intends them to have. The most important thing that we surrender is our own self—our desire to control our lives. Of course, we don't surrender and go into a vacuum. We surrender something in order to cling to God only. Surrender is the means to enjoying more fully the most beautiful thing in our lives—our joyous love relationship with God.

I decided to include this section in this book after an experience I had. Because I take an afternoon nap I usually stay up working until rather late at night. One day I was feeling unusually tired and decided that I would go to bed early. I shut down my computer, and just as I was getting ready for bed, our phone rang. It was for my wife, and the person calling seemed to be quite upset. Well, the call went on for about forty-five minutes, and because I could hear my wife talking, I could not sleep. I was getting angrier and angrier over the spoiling of my plans to go to sleep early.

After the call was over, my wife and I were discussing the problem, and I concluded, "The biggest problem is that X has not learned to surrender these things to God." Immediately I realized that I was fuming at that time because I had not surrendered my desire to sleep early to God. Because of that I had no joy in the midst of this annoying experience.

In my years in Youth for Christ (YFC) I have often had to change my plans because of needs in the ministry. Some of these plans I had to surrender were things I had eagerly waited for. Let me share one of these. While I was still in seminary, just before starting my job as leader of YFC/Sri Lanka in July 1976, I studied the book of Acts over a period of about three months. I was going to lead an evangelistic community, and here we had a good model for us to follow. I came back to Sri Lanka and taught the things I had learned from Acts and tried to implement them in our ministry and later in the church that my wife and I helped restart (after its attendance had dropped to zero).

I soon began to feel that I should write a book on Acts someday. I decided that I would write this book after at least fifteen years of trying to apply Acts in our ministry in YFC and the church. But when that time came, I had despaired of getting publishers to take on books of Bible exposition. I did not start writing, but I kept studying Acts and preparing new studies from it. Then around 1994 I got a fax from Zondervan asking me whether I would consider writing the volume on Acts in their NIV Application Commentary series. I couldn't believe my eyes. We had a YFC board meeting about two days after I got that fax. I presented the proposal to the board and asked for a sabbatical, which was granted. I was thrilled and was eagerly looking forward to taking this break to do what I love so much—studying the Word. As we felt that our children would find it difficult to adjust back to Sri Lanka if we went abroad at this stage of their lives, we decided to stay at home for the sabbatical.

Just before the sabbatical started, we found out that Colombo Theological Seminary, of which I was board chairman, would soon be without a principal (president). The school was only two years old. It could not survive without a principal. The board asked me whether I would take on the job. I felt God wanted me to do this, and I got permission from the YFC board to do so. I still feel like crying when I think of that year! I had a goal of studying forty hours a week and working in the seminary fifteen to twenty hours. I fell short of the forty hours almost every week, but I finished the 650-page commentary. And I think the Lord has blessed that book. I even think it was a better book because of the strain that went into writing it!

Often the things we have to surrender are not easy to give up—things like our health, our convenience, our comfort, or our reputation. As my wife and I get older, I often wish that we could die around the same time. But the law of averages says that that is unlikely. My wife says it would be better for me to die first because she knows how lost I would be without her. We know that one of us will have to surrender the one who dies first. If through surrender we are willing to accept the possibility of this deeply sorrowful parting, we can prepare for it constructively. The surrender will hopefully be an affirmation that no one, not even our beloved spouse, will take the place of supreme importance that God has in our lives. Then, amidst the deep sorrow of the parting, we could still cling to God and know the glad sorrow of his comforting presence with those he loves.

For a biblical Christian, rather than being something to dread, surrender can become the gateway to an exciting adventure. We know that God will bring something good out of every situation. Even as we go through pain, this truth sustains us and we wonder, "How will God do it this time?" We anticipate his deliverance with holy longing. And when we see what he has done, our joy is complete!

Chapter Seven

NOT GLUTTONS FOR PUNISHMENT

Reading what I have said so far could give you the impression that I am advocating a morbid desire to suffer. Some fathers of the early church acted in this way. But surely that is not a biblical attitude. I have heard people say that full-time Christian workers do not need to be paid salaries like those in "secular" jobs because suffering is an aspect of Christian service, and when they joined the ministry they made a decision that includes suffering of this kind. The Bible, however, is clear that Christian workers must be paid an adequate salary so they will be able to concentrate on their ministry unhindered by the burden of financial constraints (1 Cor. 9:3-14; 1 Tim. 5:17).

We do not go after suffering. In fact, if something unjust happens, we may need to protest about it, especially if an important principle is at stake. Paul was arrested and given a public beating in Philippi, a thing that should not have been done to a Roman citizen.

So when the officials there released him, he did not just leave. He protested about the illegal way he had been treated (Acts 16:37). This caused considerable alarm among the officials. He needed to do that for the protection of other Christians. In fact, much of the book of Acts was written in a way that would defend Christianity and give it legal legitimacy.

Today as opposition to the gospel grows, much wisdom is needed to discern when we should turn the other cheek and when we should stand up for our right to practice Christianity. Once when the great Indian evangelist Sundar Singh was preaching on the banks of a holy river, someone threw sand into his eyes. The other Hindu holy men who were there got angry that a preacher was treated in that way, and they got hold of the man and were taking him to a policeman. Sundar Singh, returning after washing off the mud from his eyes, saw what was happening and immediately went and pleaded on behalf of the man. He secured his release and went on preaching. The stunned man, Vidyananda, was so impressed that he not only begged Sundar Singh's forgiveness but also became a seeker after the truth and accompanied him on his journeys.[1] In that case turning the other cheek was the Christian thing to do.

A different kind of reaction was needed in Sri Lanka when a convert to Christianity who was living in a predominantly Buddhist village died. The village leaders said that he could not be buried in the village cemetery because he had given up Buddhism. On that occasion the Christians worked really hard, speaking to political leaders and government officials, to secure the right to bury Christians in the village cemetery. This right was secured, and an important precedent was set that would help Christians in the future.

The gospel was defended in both these incidents. The first one did so by demonstrating the Christian principle of loving our enemies. The second did so by helping win the legitimate right of Christians to enjoy the services that are open to all citizens of Sri Lanka.

So we do not go after suffering. But when suffering comes to us, we know that it will be used by God to be a blessing to us. The English word *blessing* is derived from the old English *bledsian*, which is related to the word *blood*. It comes from the use of blood in sacrifice. Blessing comes through sacrifice. Because of that, Christians who suffer for their principles consider it an honor to do so. Paul said, "For it has been granted to you that for the sake of Christ you should not only believe in him but also suffer for his sake" (Phil. 1:29). The Greek word translated "granted" (*charizomai*) means "to give graciously." J. B. Lightfoot in his comment on this verse says, "God has granted to you the high privilege of suffering for Christ; this is the surest sign, that He looks upon you with favour."[2] This is why when the authorities "beat [the apostles] and charged them not to speak in the name of Jesus, and let them go . . . they left the presence of the council, rejoicing that they were counted worthy to suffer dishonor for the name" (Acts 5:40-41).

Peter Kuzmic is one of the world's leading missiologists today. His father was a Pentecostal pastor in the former Yugoslavia. The authorities came and destroyed the building of the church of which he was pastor. They imprisoned him for a time. Then they would get him to make two visits a day to the security office, which was quite a distance from his home. When he went, they would hit him so hard that his cheeks would be so swollen he was unable to eat. Kuzmic says that he remembers his father telling his wife, amidst the pain, about what a privilege it was to suffer for Christ and to have them do to him what they did to Jesus.

The attitude we have described thus far in this book is illustrated well in a story that Norman Grubb told about his father-in-law, C. T. Studd. Studd was the founder of the Heart of Africa Mission, now known as WEC International. For much of his missionary career he lived deep in the jungles of Africa. Norman Grubb lived with him for some time. He says that the mail would come once every two weeks, and Studd made quite a ritual of the opening of the mail.

Once a lot of funds came in the mail, and Studd said, "Bless God forever! He knows what a bunch of grumblers we are and he has sent enough to keep us quiet." Another time, when a small amount came in, Studd said, "Hallelujah, we must be growing in grace. He thinks we are learning to trust him." Once nothing came in. Studd's response was, "Hallelujah, praise God forever! We are in the kingdom already, for in the kingdom there is neither eating nor drinking, but righteousness, joy and peace in the Holy Ghost."[3]

We detect a tinge of humor here. But we must not miss the demonstration of unflinching belief in the sovereignty of God that looks at every trial in a positive light.

Chapter Eight

A THEOLOGICAL BLIND SPOT?

The church in each culture has its own special challenges—theological blind spots that hinder Christians from growing to full maturity in Christ. I think the most serious blind spot in the Asian church is communicating the biblical truth that though "God is love" (1 John 4:8, 16), he requires personal accountability for our actions. In our shame-based cultures, being open about one's sins is culturally unacceptable, and therefore spiritual accountability is difficult to foster.

I think one of the most serious theological blind spots in the western church is a defective understanding of suffering. There seems to be a lot of reflection on how to avoid suffering and on what to do when we hurt. We have a lot of teaching about escape from and therapy for suffering, but there is inadequate teaching about the theology of suffering. Christians are not taught why they should expect suffering as followers of Christ and why suffering is so important for healthy growth as a Christian. So suffering is viewed only in a negative way.

The "good life," comfort, convenience, and a painless life have become necessities that people view as basic rights. If they do not have these, they think something has gone wrong. So when something like inconvenience or pain comes, they do all they can to avoid or lessen it. One of the results of this attitude is a severe restriction of spiritual growth, for God intends us to grow through trials.

Later we will see that it is commitment to people that causes much pain in our lives. Many church structures are fashioned so as to not leave much room for such pain. There isn't an opportunity for people to grow uncomfortably close to each other and get frustrated with each other. Sometimes small groups within the church are advertised in such a way as to assure prospective participants that the commitment required is minimal. A course of study will be held for three months, and then they could join another group. One sad result of this is that many Christians do not have an opportunity to develop ties of spiritual accountability with other Christians, ties that are vital for Christian growth. So this defective theology results in a stunting of growth.

A second result of not having a proper theology of suffering is that we suffer more than we need to when we encounter pain or frustration. Living as we do in this fallen world, we can be certain that we will encounter suffering. It is so closely embedded into life on earth that no human can avoid it. If believers do not accept suffering as something out of which good will come, when they suffer they think something is seriously wrong. The comments of others can often reinforce that idea. They get disillusioned with God and the church, or they struggle with unnecessary discouragement and doubt. You cannot have joy with such attitudes.

A third result of not having a proper theology of suffering is that some who face suffering can move away from a tough call to something that looks easier. But in the process they move away from God's best for them and become much less effective from an eternal perspective. A couple called to work with a resistant people group may not see any visible fruit for several years. They will find the frustration of such seemingly fruitless ministry difficult to endure, especially because those supporting their ministry are expecting some measurable results. Unable to handle this frustration, they may go to another place that seems to be more ideally suited for them. But God may want them to endure where they are.

Or perhaps a brilliant preacher who has preached for many years to a small congregation of Muslim converts and inquirers returns to his homeland to become pastor of a congregation of several thousand members. It would seem that his gifts are used so much more effectively in his new sphere of service. But the witness of history is that God sent some of the greatest minds in the church to the hardest places. Some of the most brilliant people in the church need to devote themselves to developing strategies to reach the most resistant people. But our lopsided understanding of fulfillment and gifts makes setting apart such people for this work very difficult to justify today.

We have seen a sad phenomenon taking place with Sri Lankans who come back after studying abroad with good theological qualifications. They seem to be looking for the ideal package where they can be most fulfilled in using their gifts and where they have a salary that suits their qualifications. They don't come to die for our people. It is scandalous but true that even in the church what was once viewed as selfishness has become acceptable and even respectable.

Sri Lanka is too poor a country to afford people who will devote themselves exclusively to their areas of giftedness. The body within which a person serves may often ask a person to do things that seem to take them away from their primary callings. Because Christianity is a religion where the needs of the body as a whole become our personal needs, a biblical Christian will submit to the will of the body. People who have become used to the radical individualism of affluent countries will find such submission to the body difficult to endure.

So some of these talented and qualified people end up leaving Sri Lanka after a few years of service and going to countries where they think they can use their gifts in a better way and where they are remunerated for their service more substantially. Often the need in the countries they leave is incomparably greater than the need in the country to which they go.

Others start their own organizations where they can develop their own job description according to what they think are their gifts and where they do not have to submit to the will of a wider body. Still others become consultants in their area of expertise, imparting their specialized knowledge to various groups without having to submit to and be accountable to one group.

I have not yet quoted any Scriptures in this study. If there was one Scripture I would like to quote, it is the whole book of Second Corinthians. It starts with a reference to a severe affliction that Paul and his companions experienced: "For we do not want you to be ignorant, brothers, of the affliction we experienced in Asia. For we were so utterly burdened beyond our strength that we despaired of life itself. Indeed, we felt that we had received the sentence of death" (1:8-9a). In this epistle we find five other listings of severe suffering (4:8-12; 6:4-5, 8-10; 11:23-28, 32-33). It is in this letter that Paul talks about his thorn in the flesh, which he described as "a messenger of Satan to harass me" (12:1-10).

Yet despite all this focus on suffering, the overwhelming theme of 2 Corinthians is *The Glory of the Ministry: Paul's Exultation in Preaching*, which is the title of a book of expositions on this epistle by A. T. Robertson.[1] Paul had a theology of suffering that helped him see a silver lining in all his suffering. For example, his conclusion to his experience of unanswered prayer regarding his thorn in the flesh was, "For when I am weak, then I am strong" (12:10b). This silver-lining approach to suffering is well expressed in a list of paradoxical affirmations Paul makes in this epistle:

> . . . *through honor and dishonor,*
> *through slander and praise.*
> *We are treated as impostors, and yet are true;*
> *as unknown, and yet well known;*
> *as dying, and behold, we live;*

as punished, and yet not killed;
as sorrowful, yet always rejoicing;
as poor, yet making many rich;
as having nothing, yet possessing everything. (2 Cor. 6:8-10)

That's the attitude that a biblically grounded theology of suffering produces in a Christian. As we said earlier, the happiest people in the world are not those who have no suffering—they are those who are not afraid of suffering.

Part Two

SUFFERING BRINGS US NEARER TO CHRIST

. . . and in my flesh I am filling up what is lacking in Christ's afflictions . . .

COLOSSIANS 1:24B

Chapter Nine

THE FELLOWSHIP OF SUFFERING

In Colossians 1:24 Paul gives two reasons why we can rejoice in suffering: "Now I rejoice in my sufferings for your sake, and in my flesh I am filling up what is lacking in Christ's afflictions for the sake of his body, that is, the church." Paul rejoices, first, because he fills up what is lacking in Christ's afflictions and, second, because the suffering is for the sake of the church.

What a strange statement Paul makes here! He says, "In my flesh I am filling up what is lacking in Christ's afflictions." Surely Paul, the one who taught so deeply about the sufficiency of Christ, could not be saying that more needed to be done to complete the sacrifice of Christ. The many interpretations of this statement can basically be divided into two groups.

The first group understands this statement as meaning that there is a quota of suffering that still needs to be endured to complete the work that arose as a result of Christ's death. Some say this suffering was needed so that the results of the work of Christ could be appropriated by people. That is, though the work of Christ is complete, the reception of the message of his sufferings is not complete. Paul wanted to take on the quota of suffering that was needed to be borne so that the gospel would go out to the world. Others say that Paul was talking about the quota of suffering that was needed for the church to endure (sometimes called the messianic woes) before the end of time comes and Christ returns to the earth.

There is a strong case for this general view, and it is held by several great New Testament scholars. I, however, think the other view has more to commend it because it is consistent with a lot of Paul's teaching on suffering. It was held by older scholars like John Calvin and Matthew Henry. In recent times David Garland[1] is among those who have held it. According to this view, what Paul wants to fill up is his own experience of Christ's suffering. Christ is a suffering Savior, and if we are to follow him or be like him, we must suffer like he did. Paul expresses this as a desire when he says elsewhere, ". . . that I may know him and the power of his resurrection, and may share his sufferings, becoming like him in his death" (Phil. 3:10). Peter O'Brien points out that Paul is saying here that experiencing the power of Christ's resurrection and sharing in his sufferings are aspects of knowing Christ.[2]

Paul uses the familiar word *koinōnia* in Philippians 3:10, and the literal translation is, "the fellowship of his sufferings." There is a depth of oneness with Christ that we can experience only through suffering. Paul discovered this right at the start of his Christian life when he heard Jesus say, "Saul, Saul, why are you persecuting me?" (Acts 9:4). He was assaulting the church, but guess who was feeling the pain? The church and Christ had become so united in suffering that when Paul hit the church, he was actually hitting Christ. Later Paul would expound in depth about what it means to be "in Christ." In describing our inheritance in Christ, Paul said, ". . . if children, then heirs—heirs of God and fellow heirs with Christ, provided *we suffer with him* in order that we may also be glorified with him" (Rom. 8:17, emphasis added). When we suffer, we are suffering with Christ.

What if our greatest desire in life is to get close to Jesus and we recognize that suffering will help us achieve our ambition? If so, suffering won't be a big deal to us. It would be something like the trouble one goes through in order to pass an exam or win a gold medal at the Olympic Games. Toyohiko Kagawa (1888–1960) was a Japanese evangelist and social reformer about whom we will say more later. At one time he thought he was going blind (though this did not happen). He responded to this prospect by saying, "The darkness, the darkness is a holy of holies of which no one can rob me. In the darkness I meet God face to face."[3]

A Chinese evangelist who spent many years in prison because of his faith said, "If you accept suffering for your faith as a privilege, it becomes your friend and brings you closer to God."[4] A Romanian pastor who also suffered under Communist rule said, "Christians are like nails; the harder you hit them, the deeper they go."[5]

When Sadhu Sundar Singh became a Christian as a teenager, he was poisoned by his brothers and kicked out of his home. After being miraculously healed, he devoted himself to proclaiming the gospel. Once he was preaching near his family home, and he decided to visit his father. It broke his heart when his father treated him like an outcast. He made his son sit at a distance so he would not pollute the family or their vessels. When he gave his son water, he poured it onto his hands, keeping the jug high above him.

This is how Sundar Singh responded: "When I saw this treatment I could not restrain the tears flowing from my eyes that my father, who used to love me so much, now hated me as if I was untouchable." Yet amidst this pain Sundar experienced the fellowship of sharing in Christ's suffering. He says, "In spite of all this, my heart was filled with inexpressible peace. I thanked him for this treatment also . . . and respectfully I said good-bye, and went away. In the fields, I prayed and thanked God, and then slept under a tree, and in the morning continued my way."[6] Sundar Singh's father became a Christian shortly before his death.[7]

Enjoying intimacy with Christ is the sweetest and most satisfying experience in life. One who realizes this would be willing to lose anything that is necessary to give up in order to deepen that intimacy. John and Betty Stam, missionaries in China, were killed by the Communists in 1934 when they were twenty-seven and twenty-eight years old. John once said, "Take away everything I have, but do not take away the sweetness of walking and talking with the king of glory."[8]

If we have such a desire for intimacy with Christ, when we know that suffering deepens this intimacy, suffering loses its sting. We do not fear it. Instead, when it comes we choose to turn it into an opportunity to achieve our ambition—to get nearer to Christ. Graham Kendrick expresses this desire to know Jesus well in a song he wrote:

> All I once held dear, built my life upon,
> All this world reveres and wars to own;
> All I once thought gain I have counted loss,
> Spent and worthless now compared to this.
>
> Knowing you, Jesus, knowing you
> There is no greater thing.
> You're my all, you're the best,
> You're my joy, my righteousness,
> And I love you, Lord.
>
> Now my heart's desire is to know you more,
> To be found in you and known as yours,
> To possess by faith what I could not earn
> All surpassing gift of righteousness.
>
> Oh to know the power of your risen life,
> And to know you in your sufferings;
> To become like you in your death, my Lord,
> So with you to live and never die.[9]

Chapter Ten

BECOMING LIKE CHRIST

Graham Kendrick's song with which we ended the last meditation ended like this:

> To become like you in your death, my Lord,
> So with you to live and never die.

These words point to another aspect of how suffering brings us nearer to Jesus—it helps us become like Christ.

Some years ago I went through the New Testament looking for all the instances where Jesus is presented as a model to follow. I found some general statements like, "Be imitators of me, as I am of Christ" (1 Cor. 11:1). I found a few places where we are asked to forgive and be patient just as he was patient (Eph. 4:32; Col 3:13). Jesus himself asks us to follow his example of washing the feet of the disciples (John 13:14)—that is, serving one another. Most of the references, however, were about following Christ's example of suffering.

One of the best known texts about following Christ's example is Hebrews 12:1-2 where we are asked to "run with endurance the race that is set before us, looking to Jesus, the founder and perfecter of our faith." We often stop with that and forget that what we are asked to do is to suffer like Jesus. This sentence goes on to say, ". . . who for the joy that was set before him endured the cross, despising the shame, and is seated at the right hand of the throne of God" (Heb. 12:2b).

Now even though we know that Jesus rose from the dead with a great triumph, it is not easy to follow him to death, especially with all the prosperity theology that people are exposed to today. We hear popular TV preachers say that because Christ has taken on the curse on our behalf, we are freed from the effects of the curse and therefore we should not suffer. Those who trustingly accept suffering without fighting it are accused of having little faith. Peter has something to say to this situation: "Since therefore Christ suffered in the flesh, arm yourselves with the same way of thinking" (1 Pet. 4:1). We are bombarded with ideas that claim that when we suffer, it is because we are doing something wrong. But God asks us to arm ourselves with the thinking of Christ, who suffered in the flesh. He faced physical suffering, and so must we. So we should begin to think about suffering like Christ did and face it looking for good to come out of it.[1]

We looked at Paul's statement in Philippians 3:10 that he wants to "share his [Christ's] sufferings." He expands this statement by going on to say, "becoming like him in his death." The verb translated "becoming like" here is *summorphizō*. It means "to cause to be similar in form or style to something else."[2] When we suffer with Christ, we become like him.

The same thought is given in the familiar text Romans 8:28-29: "And we know that for those who love God all things work together for good, for those who are called according to his purpose. For those whom he foreknew he also predestined to be conformed to the image of his Son, in order that he might be the firstborn among many brothers." The good that comes out of all our experiences is that we will become what God intended when he predestined us: being conformed to the image of Christ.

Paul goes on to say that when that happens, Jesus becomes our firstborn (Rom. 8:29b). But was he not always "the firstborn among many brothers"? He is our elder brother; but if we do not behave like him, he does not seem to be so. We are at that time not who we are meant to be, and that would mean that we are restless, not fully experiencing what it means to be a brother of Christ. But when we become like him, he truly becomes our brother, and we become what we were made to be. That means that we experience the *shalom*—the wholeness—that God intended us to have when he created us.

Stephen demonstrated what it means to become like Christ in suffering when he was being killed. His opponents "were enraged, and they ground their teeth at him" (Acts 7:54). But at that time Stephen was experiencing the fellowship of suffering with Christ in a most powerful manner: "But he, full of the Holy Spirit, gazed into heaven and saw the glory of God, and Jesus standing at the right hand of God" (v. 55). The opponents proceeded to begin the execution of Stephen by stoning. Then Stephen, who was experiencing the fellowship of suffering through the nearness of Christ, began to do what Jesus did when he was executed: "And as they were stoning Stephen, he called out, 'Lord Jesus, receive my spirit.' And falling to his knees he cried out with a loud voice, 'Lord, do not hold this sin against them.' And when he had said this, he fell asleep" (vv. 59-60).

The people did to Stephen what they did to Christ. He experienced the nearness of Christ at that time, and he began to do the same things that Christ did when he died.

A man in China named Chang Men went blind in his thirties and was known as Blind Chang. But he was given a nickname, *Wu so pu wei te*, which summed up what people thought of him. It meant "one without a particle of good in him." His neighbors believed that he had been struck blind as a punishment for his wicked lifestyle. He had thrown his wife and daughter out of his home; he gambled, stole, and was a womanizer. But then he heard that blind people were being cured in a mission hospital and went there for treatment. There he not only partially received physical sight but, better yet, received spiritual sight by responding to the gospel.

Blind Chang wanted to be baptized, but he was told that a missionary would come to his village and do that for him. The missionary came five months later, and he discovered that four hundred people wanted to become Christians because of Blind Chang's witness. He went to a local hospital and had an operation, hoping to improve his eyesight further, but became fully blind as a result. Blind Chang then became an itinerant evangelist. He could quote almost the whole New Testament and many chapters of the Old Testament by heart.

Then came the Boxer Rebellion at the turn of the twentieth century when people associated with the West were attacked. Hundreds of missionaries and thousands of Christians died. In one place fifty Christians were arrested, and their captors planned to kill them. But they were told that for each Christian they killed, ten more would appear. Therefore they decided to kill the ringleader of the Christians, Blind Chang. The prisoners were asked where they could find him. But no Christian was willing to betray him. One of these prisoners was able to escape, and he found Chang and told him what was going on.

Chang went at once to the Boxers. He was ordered to worship their god of war in a temple, but he refused to do that. He was put in an open cart and paraded through the town on their way to the cemetery outside town. While going through the town, Chang sang a song:

Jesus loves me, he who died
Heaven's gate to open wide;
He will wash away my sin,
Let his little child come in.

Jesus loves me, he will stay,
Close beside me all the way;
If I love him, when I die,
He will take me home on high.

Chang was decapitated by a sword. The last words he said were, "Heavenly Father, receive my spirit."[3]

Can you see how suffering made him like Jesus? When he saw that his flock was in trouble, he did not run away to hide in a place of safety, like a hired hand. He died for the sheep, like the Good Shepherd (see John 10:11-15). As Chang died he sang of the nearness of Jesus and the anticipation of being welcomed into heaven by him. And the last words he said were much like the last words of Jesus before he died.

Chapter Eleven

MOTIVES PURIFIED

Most servants of God try to serve out of the pure motive of doing all for the glory of God, but it is very difficult to know when our motives are pure and when they are selfish. We want to do the best possible job in all that we do for God. But why do we want to do that? Is it only because we want God to be glorified, or is there a tinge of selfish ambition that wants us to be better than others—a motivation that is not worthy of the gospel?

Because it is so hard for us to be totally and solely God-honoring in all we do, God often allows us to go through a discipline of some sort that helps purify our motives. In Hebrews 12:3-11 there is an extended discussion on how God disciplines those whom he loves so they will grow in grace.

James also teaches this, saying, "Count it all joy, my brothers, when you meet trials of various kinds, for you know that the testing of your faith produces steadfastness" (James 1:2-3). Trials test our faith. The testing analogy comes from the practice of testing metals in the fire, thus purifying them of impurities. The process also reveals what impurities existed in the metal.

Recently I gave a two-part series of messages at an international conference. During my first talk there was a little confusion about the time allocated to me. While speaking I realized that I had to rush my talk to finish on time. Foolishly, I began to speak fast. The first language of many in the audience was not English, and they found it hard to follow what I was saying. My tense mood also caused me to lose my sense of freedom as I spoke. After I finished, I realized the message had not been well understood. After the talk was over, some friends who were there and were concerned that I had not done a good job gave me advice on how I should give my next talk.

I went to my room quite devastated. There is nothing I dread in life as much as ministering without the freedom of knowing that I am being carried along by the Spirit's anointing. I clearly had not sensed this that evening. I sent a text message to my wife asking her to call me, and I told her what had happened. I asked her to inform my friends to pray about my next session the next morning. I also asked her to pray for me over the phone. That night I worked hard on cutting short my second message so I would not be rushed. The next morning's session went really well. The same friends who had advised me the night before came and expressed their joy over their feeling that God had used that talk.

As I was thinking about this, I was trying to make sense of what had happened. I realized that during the first few days of the conference many people had come up to me and told me how much they had appreciated my books and talks I had given at various conferences. I realized that I had become proud. I wanted my talks at this conference to be outstanding. But my motivation had shifted from wanting to glorify Christ to wanting people to see my abilities as a speaker and Bible teacher. Such motivation resulted in my ministering out of my own strength, for God will not share his glory with another. If such attitudes grew within me, my ministry would be displeasing to God, and his anointing would leave me.

God graciously permitted me to make a mess of my talk so he could purify my motives. I thanked God for the chastisement and gave myself a mental slap on the cheek, saying, "Thanks, Lord, I needed that!" I asked him to help me, despite the impurity of my motives, to seek only his glory in all I do.

It is sad that most of the unpleasantness that we experience among Christians is because some are acting with impure motives. A Christian has been hurt, and he won't rest until he feels he has been justified and until those who hurt him have been shown to be wrong. Sometimes unpleasantness comes because of the ambition some have for a position in the church. The way elections for prominent church offices are conducted in some parts of the world is amazing! People are given bribes to vote for a candidate. Underhanded methods are used so one candidate will have an advantage. Scandalous stories are spread about opposing candidates. People go to court over technicalities and don't seem to mind that the name of Christ is coming into disrepute as Christians fight among each other in front of the world. I shudder to think what will happen to these people at the judgment!

Albert Osburne was the most famous hymn-writer of the Salvation Army. When he was a young officer in London, revival spread in the area where he had been leading. Following this revival an officer came and told him that he heard that the leaders were planning to divide his district. He urged Osburne not to let it happen. He said that God was blessing his district so much and to divide the district would hinder the work of God. The officer told him, "I think you ought to fight it." Osburne replied, "Oh, no. I want to do the will of God and respect my superiors. I will not do that."

However, Osburne began to argue about this with the leadership. Later he said that the real reason for his arguing was because he now had less prestige and power. "Unwittingly I had begun to fight not for the kingdom but for my position in the kingdom, and the Holy Spirit was grieved." He added, "When the Spirit grieves, the Spirit leaves." He said he went through the motions of ministry, but there was a distance between him and God. Deadness had entered his life, and he felt empty inside.

Then Osburne had a car crash, and he had a long recovery. God began to work on him. One day he heard some singing in the room next to his in the hospital. He said, "I heard them sing of the glories of God. My heart began to yearn once again for that kind of intimacy with God. I wept my heart out in repentance. God forgave me. And the Spirit came and filled my heart afresh." Thank God, Osburne ended his life well. He is much loved as a hymn-writer to this day.[1]

Chapter Twelve

SHAME AND HONOR

One of the hardest aspects of the suffering of Christians is enduring shame. I am presently reading the book of Job for my devotions. As I read the speeches of his four friends and try to put myself in Job's shoes, I think I would have found the shame Job endured unbearable! If when we suffer people appreciate the sacrifices we make and admire us for our commitment, the sacrifice becomes a little more bearable. But it is much harder if they think we are suffering because of our folly or that we are being punished for doing wrong even though we ourselves refuse to admit to wrongdoing.

Hebrews 13:12-13 says that our model for suffering shame is Jesus: "So Jesus also suffered outside the gate in order to sanctify the people through his own blood. Therefore let us go to him outside the camp and bear the reproach he endured." We must never forget that just as the means used by Christ to win our salvation was shameful, those who serve Christ will also invariably face shame.

The readers of the letter to the Hebrews were asked to "go to

[Christ] outside the camp." Just as the Jews rejected Jesus and cast him out, these Christians would face the rejection of their own people. This is something that many Christians face today. We Sri Lankan Christians love our nation. We have chosen to stay in our nation without availing ourselves of offers to live abroad despite huge problems in the country. When our country wins at cricket, we are as excited as anyone else. Yet we are accused of being the stooges of foreign powers who are trying to conquer our nation (through economic and military power) like so-called Christian nations did in the past. We love our nation and are willing to suffer for its welfare, but we are called traitors to our nation. This is very painful!

I am constantly amazed by the fact that when possibly the greatest hero in church history—Paul—was on trial in Rome toward the end of his life, no one from the Roman church was there to support him. I think 2 Timothy 4:16 is one of the most tragic verses in the whole Bible: "At my first defense no one came to stand by me, but all deserted me. May it not be charged against them!"

Yet today, twenty centuries later, the shame is not Paul's; it belongs to those who deserted him. It was said of Jesus, ". . . who for the joy that was set before him endured the cross, despising the shame, and is seated at the right hand of the throne of God" (Heb. 12:2). He despised the shame because he knew there would be joy in the end. The verb "despising" or "scorning" (NIV) is a strong one. He didn't endure the shame with difficulty—he treated it with disdain—because he was sure of the glorious end.

And we can do the same as we suffer shame because of faithfulness to Christ. In John 12 Jesus talked about how he would be glorified through his death, and then he challenged his followers also to bear fruit by dying like a grain of wheat (John 12:23-25). Then he talked of the fellowship that we can have with him in suffering: "If anyone serves me, he must follow me; and where I am, there will my servant be also" (v. 26a). Then he described the honor that comes from serving God: "If anyone serves me, the Father will honor him" (v. 26b). Honor will come in God's time.

Sometimes honor is given to us during our lifetime, as happened with Job. But we can be sure that honor always awaits the faithful at the judgment. An important factor that helps us endure shame is the prospect of honor at the judgment. Actually the doctrine of judgment is something that helps us avoid bitterness as we serve Jesus in a fallen world.[1] As we see dishonorable and unjust people succeed while we are humiliated by relative failure despite our faithfulness to our call, it is easy to get bitter.

There is within us a sense of justice that says good should be rewarded and evil punished. When we see the opposite, it is right to be angry. But we do not need to experience bitterness that destroys our joy and makes us ineffective in God's service. Sadly, many honest servants of God struggle with severe anger because of the injustice of which they seem to be victims. This makes them emotional and spiritual cripples. They must remember that the final chapter has not been written on their life.

A missionary who had served God faithfully for several years was returning home to the United States on the same ship on which the President was returning after a short visit to Africa. There was an impressive welcome for the President, but no one had come to welcome the missionary. He felt very hurt by this and complained to God that when the President comes home from a short trip he is welcomed with much fanfare, but when the missionary comes home after so many years of sacrificial service there is no welcome for him. Then he sensed God telling him, "But you have not come home yet."[2]

Paul said, "For this light momentary affliction is preparing for us an eternal weight of glory beyond all comparison" (2 Cor. 4:17). Actually his many listings of suffering in 2 Corinthians, including the list in this passage (vv. 8-16), show that what he encountered was very severe suffering. But in comparison to the glory that awaits us, even such severe suffering can only be described as "slight momentary affliction."

Amy Carmichael (1867–1951) was one of the great missionary

heroines of the last century. She rescued scores of children in India who had been sold by their parents to a life of degradation in the temples. She then gave them a happy home to grow up in. She once said, "We have all eternity to celebrate our victories, but only a few hours before sunset to win them."

So thinking about the honor that comes in the future helps us in two ways. First, we lose our reason for being bitter about the prosperity of the wicked, and second, we are motivated to pay the price of service. If we don't teach Christians about heaven and hell and the judgment, we should not be surprised if only a few devoted believers who are willing to pay the price emerge from our ministries. With money and good planning we can develop big and impressive programs. But we would not produce an army that will serve God and pay the price to reap a truly long-lasting harvest.

Chapter Thirteen

SOLIDARITY WITH CHRIST

Few heroes in missionary history suffered as much as the medical doctor David Livingstone (1813–1873). It is said that even
during the most severe periods of anti-western sentiment in Africa,
people always had a good word to say about Livingstone. He was an
explorer who opened up the interior of Africa to the outside world.
And he had two aims in doing that. The first was to open the interior
so missionaries could take the gospel to the people there. The second
was to open Africa to legitimate trade so the horrible slave-trading
in human flesh would end. His reports had a big part to play in the
abolition of slavery in the western world.[1]

His hand was bitten and maimed by a lion. His wife died on
the field. He was often alone in his travels. The one house he built
was burned. And often his body would be wracked by dysentery
and fever. Someone once told him that he had sacrificed a lot for
the gospel. His response was, "Sacrifice? The only sacrifice is to

live outside the will of God." He was asked what helped him go on despite so much hardship. He said that always ringing in his ears, even when he was terribly sick, were the words of Jesus, "Lo, I am with you always, even unto the end of the world" (Matt. 28:20, KJV). Livingstone once said, "Without Christ not one step; with him anywhere."

In the last few chapters we have been saying that suffering brings us closer to Christ. It is the presence of Christ with us that gives us the courage to go on amidst the pain. Our God has said, "I will never leave you nor forsake you" (Heb. 13:5; cf. Josh. 1:5). John Chrysostom (c. 344/354–407) may have been the greatest preacher of the church in the first few centuries. Chrysostom was a nickname given to him by the church and means "golden mouth." He was a fearless preacher who was unafraid even to criticize the emperor, who lived in the same city, Constantinople. He did much to alleviate poverty, even selling some of the treasures of the church in order to feed the poor. Predictably there were many who did not like him.

The emperor once said he would put Chrysostom in prison for his preaching. Chrysostom responded that the Lord would go to prison with him. Then the emperor said he would take away all his possessions. Chrysostom replied, "There is no way for you to take away all that I possess. My treasures are in heaven and you cannot reach that far." Then the emperor said, "Well, I will banish you to the remotest corner of the kingdom." (Later he did banish Chrysostom to a remote island.) Chrysostom answered that the remotest spot in the world was part of his Savior's kingdom and his Lord would be there too.[2]

The presence of Christ with us as we face bitterness, hypocrisy, wickedness, and persecution is one of the things that helps us avoid bitterness ourselves. Looking at Jesus refreshes us because we see a love that is greater than all the hatred in the world! David wrote Psalm 27 when he was going through some really bad experiences. He even talked about his parents forsaking him (v. 10). His primary solution to his problems is very enlightening: "One thing have I asked of the LORD, that will I seek after: that I may dwell in the house of the LORD all the days of my life, to gaze upon the beauty of the LORD and to inquire in his temple" (v. 4). He wanted to wait in the presence of God and gaze at the beauty of God. This gaze cleans our life from the hurts inflicted on us and leaves it fresh with the glow of the love of God in the heart.

Graham Kendrick presents this idea in one of his songs:

> *O Lord, your tenderness*
> *Melting all my bitterness;*
> *O Lord, I receive your love.*
> *O Lord, your loveliness*
> *Changing all my ugliness;*
> *O Lord, I receive your love.*[3]

The refrain repeats the words "O Lord, I receive your love" twice. That repetition gives the feeling of lingering in God's presence while we are pumped up with a dose of God's tender loving care.

I have heard the statement that we must glance at our problems and gaze at Jesus. I must say that usually I end up giving more than a glance when facing a big problem. The laments in the Bible suggest that even God's great saints had to grapple for some time over the pain they were facing. However, once the lament is complete and the light of God's comfort clears our vision, we can gaze at Jesus. And that gaze refreshes us and takes away our bitterness, replacing it with the joy of knowing that God loves us so much.

Sisters Corrie and Betsie ten Boom spent several years first in a prison and then in a concentration camp during the Second World War because their family had sheltered Jews during the time Jews were being arrested and sent to extermination camps. Their mother was already dead, their father died in prison, and their brother was released after a time in prison. The two sisters suffered a lot in the concentration camp. Betsie died there. Corrie became a powerful traveling evangelist and author after her release from the camp. When they were tempted to be bitter, they would tell each other,

"Thank God for Romans 5:5." This verse says, "God's love has been poured into our hearts through the Holy Spirit who has been given to us." When they were faced with the wickedness of humans, they reminded themselves that the love of God given to them was greater than the wickedness of the world.

Betsie got sick at the camp and was very weak, even coughing up blood. She never recovered from this illness. At that time they had to spend much of the day shoveling dirt. Once she was so weak that she simply could not work. A guard saw that she was not working and asked her why. He thought her answer was insolent, and in a rage he whipped her. The skin of her neck split from the whipping, and blood began to pour out. Corrie saw this and took her shovel and went toward the guard to hit him. Betsie, seeing this, shouted, "Don't look, Corrie, look only at Jesus."

The sight of our Savior loving us enough to die for us takes away the sting of unkind acts. Solidarity with Christ not only gives us strength to face the blows we receive—it also gives us an experience of his love that banishes our bitterness.

Part Three

OUR SUFFERING HELPS THE CHURCH

. . . for the sake of his body, that is, the church.

COLOSSIANS 1:24C

Chapter Fourteen

SUFFERING AND CHURCH GROWTH

We have delved into the implications of two major affirmations about suffering and joy made in Colossians 1:24: "Now I rejoice in my sufferings for your sake, and in my flesh I am filling up what is lacking in Christ's afflictions for the sake of his body, that is, the church." The first is that suffering and joy are both essential aspects of Christianity. The second is that we are joyful in suffering because it helps us get nearer to Christ through filling up our experience of Christ's afflictions. Another reason for joy in suffering is given in this same verse. Paul says that he is joyful because his sufferings are "for the sake of [Christ's] body, that is, the church." We are happy because our suffering benefits the church.

My mentor, Robert Coleman, often says that one of the glaring omissions in modern church growth studies is the key part that suffering has played in the growth of the church. The witness of Scripture and church history is that usually before significant church growth there are some in the church, especially leaders, who suffer. This principle is well illustrated by what Paul says in 2 Corinthians 4:8-11. He shares an impressive list of some of his suffering:

We are afflicted in every way, but not crushed; perplexed, but not driven to despair; persecuted, but not forsaken; struck down, but not destroyed; always carrying in the body the death of Jesus, so that the life of Jesus may also be manifested in our bodies. For we who live are always being given over to death for Jesus' sake, so that the life of Jesus also may be manifested in our mortal flesh.

Then he says, "So death is at work in us, but life in you" (v. 12). Through the leader's experience of death the members experience life.

Today Christians in many countries have the blessing of belonging to a church with a significant number of members. But they often forget that the first witnesses who preached the gospel to their people had to pay a huge price before the church began to grow. My favorite story, of course, is that of the first Methodist missionaries who came to Sri Lanka nearly two centuries ago.

That missionary team was led by the aging Dr. Thomas Coke (1747–1814). He had already helped pioneer the Methodist work in North America with Francis Asbury. After that he helped start missions in the West Indies and Africa. He was leader of the missions department of the Methodist church in Britain, and in his mid-sixties when he announced that he wanted to go to Ceylon (the name given to Sri Lanka by foreign powers), people accused him of trying to build his personal kingdom and of becoming somewhat senile. He went to the annual conference with the proposal to take a mission to Sri Lanka, and it was rejected. But he persisted, and a few conferences later he managed to get a few young, inexperienced men and their spouses to promise to join him in the mission. He pledged all of his wealth to the venture. Then the conference finally relented.

One morning, after the two ships they were traveling in had just entered the Indian Ocean, Coke was found dead in his cabin. All the money of the mission was in Coke's name. The team now had no leader and no money! One member of the party, Benjamin Clough, remarked, "Now it is all trust." A little later the wife of another member, William Ault, died at sea. Five inexperienced missionaries landed on the shores of Sri Lanka and went to serve in four different parts of the country.

William Ault went to the eastern part of Sri Lanka. He was not in good health when he arrived. The region was just recovering from a drought and an epidemic. Despite fragile health he started learning the Tamil language that is spoken there and soon began to preach the gospel. He started a church and also began schools. For five months he was relatively healthy, and for three months he was very sick.

He died after only eight months there. But he had started eight schools and a church with about 150 members. One of the schools he started, Batticaloa Central College, is the oldest existing major school in the country. Recently a statue of him was erected in Batticaloa, the largest city in eastern Sri Lanka. Today if you travel on the main roads of eastern Sri Lanka you will find that the area is studded with Methodist churches. The Methodists are the largest Protestant group there.

Just before Ault died he wrote a hymn, and among its words are the following:

> *Asia salutes the rising day*
> *And, glad to own Messiah's sway*
> *Spreads forth her hands to God.*

Amidst the gloom of his mortal sickness he could see beyond to the day of God's visitation.

Seventeen missionaries died in the first fifty-two years of the Methodist mission in Sri Lanka. The ages when six of them died are not known. Of the other eleven, eight were under thirty years old when their lives on earth ended.[1]

This kind of story has been repeated countless numbers of

times. I think especially about the churches in Nigeria and South Korea. These two countries have some of the largest and most vibrant churches in the world today. Hundreds of missionaries have gone out from those two countries. But in the first few years of missionary activity there, Christians went through great suffering, with numerous martyrdoms.

It is significant that the word *martyr* comes from the Greek word for witness, *marturia*. To witness is to suffer. The writer of the letter to the Hebrews, referring to the heroes of the faith in chapter 11 who suffered so much because of their faith, describes them as "a cloud of witnesses" (12:1). Our suffering is a means of witness that helps the church grow.

There are several ways in which the church benefits through the suffering of Christians. We will look at some of these ways in the next few meditations. The first point we will discuss is that suffering helps create situations for the gospel to go out.

Acts records that following the martyrdom of Stephen, "there arose on that day a great persecution against the church in Jerusalem." The result was that they "were all scattered throughout the regions of Judea and Samaria, except the apostles" (Acts 8:1). Soon Luke would report that "those who were scattered went about preaching the word" (8:4). The refugees were witnessing for Christ.

Later Luke records one of the most significant events in the history of the church—the founding of the first Greek church in Antioch. This church would eventually become one of the great centers of Christianity. Significantly Luke associates this great event with the death of Stephen: "Now those who were scattered because of the persecution that arose over Stephen traveled as far as Phoenicia and Cyprus and Antioch" (11:19). He seems to say that the scattering that took place after Stephen's death was a key link in the events leading to this great leap forward in the life of the church when Christians took the message of the gospel to people outside the land of Israel.

With the benefit of hindsight Luke chose an interesting word in

Acts 8:1, 4 and 11:19 to describe the scattering of the church. It is *diaspeirō*, which is the word used for the scattering of seeds. You can imagine how these first Christians would have felt when they had to leave their beloved homeland. The children would have been perplexed and probably asked their parents why Jesus wasn't helping them if he was alive. But in Luke's eyes these early Christians didn't go as refugees—they went as missionaries. The death of Stephen and the ensuing wave of persecution created a situation that enabled the growth of the church in new and exciting ways.

A family in a totally Hindu Indian village came to Christ. Their fellow villagers told them they would be punished because they had forsaken their gods. Shortly after they were baptized, a son in the family became ill. The villagers said this was the revenge of the gods. The family came to church and asked their fellow believers to pray for the child's healing, as the honor of God's name was at stake. But the boy did not improve after the prayers. Soon he died, and they had the first Christian funeral in that village. The Christian's victory over the fear of death and the hope of resurrection from the dead were clearly proclaimed at the funeral. The villagers were very impressed by this, and that resulted in the people becoming open to the gospel. Many became Christians as a result of the death of that child.[2]

Chapter Fifteen

DEMONSTRATING THE GOSPEL

One of the most important themes of the Gospel of John is that Jesus revealed God's glory. When used of God, *glory* has the meaning of the manifestation of his greatness and worth. In his prologue John said, "And the Word became flesh and dwelt among us, and we have seen his glory, glory as of the only Son from the Father, full of grace and truth" (1:14). John also commented that through his first miracle, Jesus "manifested his glory" (2:11).

But the fullest demonstration of glory was to be at the cross, and we find the cross described in the Gospel of John in terms of glory. So Jesus at one of the crucial turning points of his ministry says, referring to his death, "The hour has come for the Son of Man to be glorified" (12:23). After that he talks about how the grain of wheat must die before fruit is borne. God's nature is best summarized as holy love (or truth and grace, as John 1:14 puts it). In Jesus' death we see his holiness demonstrated vividly as God expresses his hatred for sin by demanding the most valuable sacrifice that could ever be given—the death of the eternal Son of God. We also see God's love vividly as he sends his own Son to bear the punishment for our sin so that we may be freed from our guilt.

In the early church it was well known that martyrdom showed people the greatness of the gospel. People will soon get tired of today's seemingly meaningless lifestyle of living for oneself. They will ask whether they were made for something more sublime and meaningful. Then, as they see Christians considering their principles so important that they are willing to suffer for them, they may gain a new appreciation of the greatness of the gospel.

Around A.D. 320 Constantine was Emperor of the Western Roman Empire and Licinius of the East. Licinius, who had earlier signed an act of toleration for Christianity, now began to suppress it. He ordered his soldiers to repudiate Christianity on pain of death. In Sebaste in Armenia (now a part of Turkey) forty soldiers refused to give up Christianity. As they were good soldiers, their leader did not want to kill them. So he tried promises, threats, and beatings, but all of this failed to move the soldiers. Finally one evening they were stripped naked and taken to the middle of a frozen lake and told, "You may come ashore only when you are ready to deny your faith." To tempt them, fires were built on the shore with warm baths, blankets, clothing, and hot food and drink.

As the night deepened, thirty-nine of these men stood firm, but one came to the shore and saved his life. One of the guards who was standing on the shore was so moved by the steadfastness of the Christians that he stripped off his clothes and joined the others, making their number forty once more. By morning all were dead from exposure.[1]

One version of this story says that as they were going to the middle of the lake they sang and kept singing that they were forty soldiers who would not forsake Christ and would serve him to the end. When one left, the song said, "thirty-nine soldiers." But when the guard joined them, he went to the middle singing that they were forty soldiers. This guard saw the glory of the gospel when he saw the way the soldiers were willing to suffer for Christ.

Sociologist Rodney Stark has written a brilliant book, *The Rise of Christianity*, in which he describes how Christianity rose from a small group in Israel to the dominant force of the Roman Empire in such a short time. He presents factors that would have contributed to this great movement toward Christ. He shows that there were two great epidemics during those first few centuries. If those who were affected were cared for, there was a good chance they would survive. But often when a member of the family contracted the disease, the other family members left that person uncared for and left their homes for places not affected by the epidemic. The Christians, however, did not do this. As a result the percentage of Christians who survived was higher than non-Christians. The Christians also cared for those who were left behind by family members. Stark points out that the willingness to suffer in order to care for the sick had a part to play in large numbers of people in the Roman Empire turning to Christ.[2]

Evangelicals today are a despised group who are considered hopelessly out of step with today's "progressive" pluralistic attitude toward religion. This is because they "arrogantly" claim absolute uniqueness for their faith. We must not forget that this doctrine was forged and upheld in the first-century Roman Empire, which was as pluralistic in its approach to religion as our society. Because of their evangelistic activity the early Christians too were despised and persecuted. But they bore the persecution with such radiant power that their response served as a great attraction to the people. We saw this with the Roman centurion who witnessed the death of Jesus and exclaimed, "Truly this man was the Son of God!" (Mark 15:39).

Is that the way the world sees us suffer for the truth of the gospel? I am afraid that they often see us as more concerned with protecting our power and prestige and fighting to restore all that rather than loving our enemies. A government captor once told a person arrested because of the gospel, "What can your God do for you now?" The Christian responded, "He can give me the strength to forgive you."

Hundreds of missionaries were killed and many missionary properties were destroyed or damaged during the Boxer Rebellion in China at the beginning of the twentieth century. An agreement was reached whereby compensation would be given to the foreigners who suffered loss. Hudson Taylor's China Inland Mission refused to take the compensation they should have received.[3] This prompted a declaration of praise with high honor given to Jesus by the Chinese governor.[4]

Suffering brings the real issues of life to the surface. In the midst of suffering you see whether what a person has lived for has served him or her well. Most people fear suffering and do much to avoid it. What if people see that the Christians have a faith that will help them face suffering joyfully? Surely they would sit up and take note. Many would be forced to consider the claims of Christ more seriously because of that.

A godly missionary served God faithfully among an unreached people group over a long period of time. He did not see anyone from that community come to Christ during his lifetime. After his death a young missionary went to take his place and was surprised to find almost all the people responding to the call of the gospel. He asked them why they did not respond during the time that great man was among them. They responded that this old missionary had told them that if they became followers of Christ they would not fear death. This impressed them, but they needed to see whether it was really true. So they waited until he died, and seeing the way he died made them all want to become Christians.

Chapter Sixteen

IDENTIFYING WITH PEOPLE

We began the last meditation by referring to the prologue to John's Gospel, especially John 1:14: "And the Word became flesh and dwelt among us, and we have seen his glory, glory as of the only Son from the Father, full of grace and truth." Among the many nuggets found in this verse is what we call the doctrine of incarnation. The great and lofty Word described at the start of the chapter became ordinary, earthly, human flesh. The dictionary defines *incarnation* as "the embodiment of a deity or spirit in some earthly form."[1] In order to save us, Jesus became like one of us.

Later, after his resurrection, Jesus told his followers, "As the Father has sent me, even so I am sending you" (John 20:21). Jesus came into the world to bring salvation to humanity, and we too must go into the world with his message of salvation. But most people who need the gospel are not like us. Therefore, just as Jesus needed to become like us to accomplish our salvation, we will need to become like them to bring their salvation. Salvation is a glorious privilege, but it also brings with it a great responsibility. Millions of people do not know the salvation that we know. We have to take the gospel to them. But because they are so different from us, identifying with them becomes a big challenge. We call this incarnational ministry.

This is how Paul describes his attempts at identifying with people:

> *For though I am free from all, I have made myself a servant to all, that I might win more of them. To the Jews I became as a Jew, in order to win Jews. To those under the law I became as one under the law . . . that I might win those under the law. To those outside the law I became as one outside the law . . . that I might win those outside the law. To the weak I became weak, that I might win the weak. I have become all things to all people, that by all means I might save some.*
>
> 1 COR. 9:19-22

The thing I find hardest in this list is Paul's statement that he became weak in order to win the weak. We all like to operate out of a position of strength, to be in control, to have things going the way we want them to go. But that is not the way of the gospel. It is quite common for people to say they are looking for a church they are comfortable with. I think that is a scandalous statement. When were churches supposed to be comfortable places? There is too much need in the world for Christians to be comfortable.

This incarnational attitude is well expressed in a story I read about a church located next to a university that wanted very much to reach out to non-Christian students in that university. One day while the pastor was preaching, a young person with very long hair, wearing extremely casual clothes and no shoes, walked into the church. He walked up the aisle and rather than sitting on one of the comfortable pews sat on the floor on the platform. An elderly leader of the church walked toward the young man, and the congregation wondered what he would do. He sat on the floor beside that young man for the rest of the service.

Isn't it interesting that when Jesus met the Samaritan woman, the first thing he did was not to introduce himself and offer to help her get out of the terrible situation she was in (she had already had five husbands and was now living with another man). Instead the first thing the Lord of the universe, the Creator of all the water in the world, told her was, "Give me a drink" (John 4:7). He asked her to help him by giving him something that he himself had created and had complete control over! He himself became weak in order to win this morally weak person who would have otherwise been intimidated by him.

Hebrews 2:18 makes a startling statement about Jesus: "For because he himself has suffered when tempted, he is able to help those who are being tempted." Just try to imagine this: the almighty and holy God is suffering when tempted! This is just one statement describing his incarnational style. Here's another stunning statement: "He humbled himself by becoming obedient to the point of death" (Phil. 2:8). The Lord of life has died. The spotless one has taken upon himself the wages of sin. Yet one of the most attractive things about Jesus to us is the fact that he knows what we go through. He can come close to us in all the experiences we have. The world needs to know that about us Christians, that we are with them in their struggles.

Today people often see Christians as those who oppose wrong. And in a world where evil has had such terrible effects we must do that in order to restore some sanity in the world. We must oppose abortion, pornography, homosexual practice, and adultery. And when we do this we are going to suffer. People will oppose us and accuse us of all sorts of wrongs. When we try to help those who are caught up in this behavior, we will suffer inconvenience and pain and even rejection from the very people we are trying to help. I pray that the world may see us suffering winsomely—not kicking and screaming about the way we are being treated but showing that to suffer for the sake of our principles is an honor and joy.

In order to suffer like this, we must view suffering as something normal to Christianity. After all, did not Jesus himself predict, "In the world you will have tribulation" (John 16:33)? Then why is it that we get so upset when something goes wrong? Why is it that we almost always conclude when someone is suffering for the gospel that this person must be doing something wrong? G. K. Chesterton said, "Jesus promised his disciples three things—that they would be completely fearless, absurdly happy and in constant trouble."[2]

Christians are people who are crazy about mission. Once we come to know Christ, we become his ambassadors in this world. We must fight prejudice, injustice, corruption, and moral decay. We must help the needy. And even more importantly, we must never forget that people without Christ are eternally lost. We must do all we can to bring them to Christ. We must constantly ask ourselves, "How can I get close to these people?" And we must be willing to pay the price to make that possible.

George Harley was a medical doctor from the USA who went as a missionary to Liberia with his pregnant wife. He had obtained his medical degree from Yale University and his Ph.D. in tropical diseases from the University of London. He served in a remote jungle area, which he reached after walking seventeen days with his pregnant wife. After five years there no one had responded to the gospel. Every week they met for worship, and the people were invited to come, but no African joined them. Then his son died. He himself had to make the coffin and carry it to the place of burial. He was all alone there except for one African who had come to help him.

As Harley was shoveling the soil onto the casket, he was overcome with grief, and he buried his face in the fresh dirt and sobbed. The African who was watching all this raised the doctor's head by the hair and looked into his face for a long time. Then he ran into the village crying, "White man, white man, he cry like one of us." At the following Sunday service the place was packed with Africans.

Harley served in Liberia for thirty-five years. His achievements in numerous fields are amazing. He produced the first accurate map of Liberia. He was given the highest award Liberia could bestow. But before all of that he had to give his son. When a bishop from his Methodist denomination pointed that out to him, his response, referring to God, was, "He had a boy too, you know."[3]

Similarly in our own nations, before people are enamored by Jesus, they will need to see us become one with them in their experiences. Here is an unbelieving husband who dislikes church but loves football. Before he comes to Christ, his believing wife, who loves church and dislikes football, may need to decide to watch football with him. She may need to study something about football so she can talk intelligently with him about it.

When I was leaving for my city, Colombo, from one of our centers, a colleague asked me whether I would take a message to a home in a village where we had some work. This was before telephones had become popular in the villages, so messages had to be taken in person. I was in a hurry as I had a meeting to attend in Colombo. But I said I would deliver the message. When I went to the village, the Buddhist family to whom I gave the message asked me to stay for a cup of tea. I said I was in a hurry and could not stay, and I left for Colombo. Word then spread through the village that the Youth for Christ director had come to the village but was too proud to have a cup of tea in a village home.

In our village culture, where hospitality is an important value, you do not visit a home and leave without having some tea. I realized that if I could not have had tea with them, I should not have come to the village at all. The village people did not understand our urban efficiency orientation. And if we want to work with such people we will have to give up some of our urban values so as not to offend them.

We are living at a time when the study of anthropology has become very popular even in the church. Anthropology can help us in our witness because it teaches us features of the culture and behavior of the people to whom we are called. But all that understanding will be useless without incarnational identification.

Identification seems to be a very inefficient path to take. The results take too long. Therefore many will conclude that it is simply too frustrating a route in our fast-paced world. Many will opt out of this kind of calling and try to do some easier work.

I used to think that the ability to live with frustration is one of the most necessary qualifications for missionary service. Now I have broadened that idea to encompass all Christian witness. People are so distant from the gospel way of thinking and living that they will not usually respond immediately to our witness. We need to be with them, to understand them and help them understand us. That is frustrating, but it will make them more open to listening sympathetically to our message. It will open the door to dynamic witness.

Chapter Seventeen

DEEPENING OUR IMPACT

A nother way in which our suffering helps the church is by deepening our impact. At different times in church history shallowness of faith threatened to cause havoc in the church. People claimed to be Christians but then did not follow the path of true discipleship. They did not take up their cross as they followed Christ. We see this problem in the church in many places today. Perhaps the best way to deepen the faith of these shallow Christians is for them to suffer.

Incredible as it may seem, even Jesus had to suffer in order that his impact might be deepened. Hebrews 5:8-9 says, "Although he was a son, he learned obedience through what he suffered. And being made perfect, he became the source of eternal salvation to all who obey him." Jesus was never disobedient, but he had to learn obedience through suffering. Jesus was never imperfect, but there is a sense in which he was made perfect through his death.

Leon Morris explains, ". . . he learned obedience by actually obeying. There is a certain quality involved when one has performed a required action—a quality that is lacking when there is only a readiness to act. Innocence differs from virtue."[1] There was a depth of obedience and a new level of maturity, of perfection, that would come to him only through suffering.

Note that Hebrews 5:8 starts with the words, "Although he was a son . . ." As Morris puts it, "The writer does not say 'because he was a son' but 'although. . . .' Jesus' stature was such that one would not have expected him to suffer."[2] Sometimes when a Christian suffers because of his or her faithfulness to Christ, people say, "You don't deserve to suffer like this." The Bible, however, states that we need to suffer so we can become great people. Our sights are set on being great for God, on being used by God to the fullest. If so, we will need to accept the suffering that is the pathway to greatness.

I cannot say that I have experienced too much suffering in my family life before or after marriage. Though I had my fair share of trials as a student, I cannot say that I really suffered before I joined the ministry. But God has called me to minister to suffering people. Since joining the ministry I have often experienced deep hurt. I now realize that I needed to experience that so I could become a better servant of Christ.

I once went through a deep crisis of rejection when a person had misinterpreted some ministry I had done at considerable personal cost. I found his actions very painful, and for a long time I struggled with bitterness over that. While on a trip to the USA I called my close Canadian friend Brian Stiller and told him about the pain I was experiencing. I will never forget one of the things he told me. He said that one day I would realize that this experience had greatly helped me become a more effective minister of Christ. Now, about fifteen years later, I can truly say this is what has happened.

Since then I have faced many more painful experiences. I know beyond a shadow of a doubt that these experiences have taught me deep truths about the Christian life and ministry that I could not have learned otherwise. I am a better minister because of them. Martin Luther is reported to have said that there are three rules for doing right theology—prayer, meditation, and spiritual trial.

A professor of music in Vienna said about one of his students, "She is a magnificent singer, and yet there is something missing in her singing. Life has been too kind to her. But if one day it happened that someone broke her heart, she would be the finest singer in Europe!"[3] Not only in full-time ministry but in all vocations suffering helps produce depth.

Dennis Kinlaw tells the story of a pastor's wife who became a genuinely committed Christian only after her husband died. She was a passionate Christian and soul-winner. Dr. Kinlaw heard that she was losing her sight, and he visited her. She said, "Dennis, you came to comfort me, didn't you?" The question was asked almost as if she were making an accusation. Kinlaw answered, "Yes." She then said, "Would you deprive me of the privilege of walking with Christ in the dark? There are secrets I can learn in the dark that I could never learn in the light."[4]

After we have been students in the school of Christ for some time we learn not to be surprised by disappointment and pain. Then when we encounter an unexpected trial that we think we don't deserve, we affirm that God has permitted it so we can become deeper people. With such an attitude we can overcome the bitterness that will surely hit us along with the disappointment.

My son has a degree in computer science. When he was a boy, one day he had made a mistake at the computer, and he seemed to be really stuck. I will never forget the joy on his face, especially because I would have taken this problem to be a very frustrating thing. He told me, "I love when things go wrong like this because then I learn a lot of new things about computers."

One of the most painful experiences in the life of a Christian who is active in helping others is that of seeing those in whom they have invested fall into serious sin. But that forces us to ask several questions, and in trying to answer those questions we learn many important truths about Christianity. Here are some of the questions we will be forced to ask:

- Where did he (or she) go wrong? Why did he do this?
- Were there some things that happened before this big sin that opened the door to his being vulnerable to temptation?
- How could he have avoided this?
- How should we discipline him?
- How can we restore him?
- How should I relate to him now?
- Who should know about this? Why should we tell this group and not another?
- How do I handle the disappointment of this?

Most of the epistles in the New Testament were written as responses to problems. In grappling with the problems, the biblical writers developed deep theology. This is true of the great writings of the early apologists (defenders of the faith) too. Many of them were written as responses to problems in the church or outside the church.

- First Corinthians shows that there was disunity in the church, serious sexual sin, Christians going to court against each other, abuses at the Lord's Table, confusion about spiritual gifts, and Christians who did not believe in the future resurrection. These prompted a book loaded with practical advice that is still very useful to Christians.
- Second Corinthians was written after Paul had experienced the severe pain of rejection by a church that he had founded. The pain of this and the comfort he received through healing prompted one of the most profound and beautiful expressions of the glory of the ministry in print.
- Galatians does not have the customary prayer at the beginning of the letter. Instead, soon after the greeting, Paul says, "I am astonished that you are so quickly deserting him who called you in the grace of Christ and are turning to a different gospel" (1:6). The people there had been lured by false teaching, and Paul's response is a brilliant example of vibrant and profound theology.

• Disunity in the church in Philippi prompted what is probably the most profound reflection on the incarnation in the Bible (Phil. 2:1-11).

We could go on to discuss the other epistles too.

There are no shortcuts to developing depth. If you want to have a deep impact on this world, you will have to suffer.

Chapter Eighteen

SUFFERING AND CREDIBILITY

Paul often presented his suffering for the gospel as a case for his credibility. He did this several times in 2 Corinthians to defend his apostleship, which was being questioned. A good example is 6:4-10, which begins, "But as servants of God we commend ourselves in every way" (v. 4a). Then he lists why he is able to commend himself. Paul's long list has three sections. First he presents ten elements of his sufferings: "by great endurance, in afflictions, hardships, calamities, beatings, imprisonments, riots, labors, sleepless nights, hunger" (vv. 4b-5). Next he presents nine elements of his holiness: "by purity, knowledge, patience, kindness, the Holy Spirit, genuine love; by truthful speech, and the power of God; with the weapons of righteousness for the right hand and for the left" (vv. 6-7). Finally he gives another list of nine elements of suffering: "through honor and dishonor, through slander and praise. We are treated as impostors, and yet are true; as unknown, and yet well known; as dying, and behold, we live; as punished, and yet not killed; as sorrowful, yet always rejoicing; as poor, yet making many rich; as having nothing, yet possessing everything" (vv. 8-10).

So Paul defended his credibility by listing nineteen kinds of suffering and nine aspects of his holiness. These are the two main means of winning the hearts of the people we lead: holiness and suffering for the cause.

Writing to the Galatians, who were being led astray by some false teachers who rejected Paul's message and position, he said, "From now on let no one cause me trouble, for I bear on my body the marks of Jesus" (6:17). Just as the "marks" or stigmata of a slave revealed who owned the slave, the scars that Paul had received from the beatings he had received bore witness to his genuineness as a slave of Christ.[1]

Paul begins the practical section of his letter to the Ephesians with the words, "I therefore, a prisoner for the Lord, urge you to walk in a manner worthy of the calling to which you have been called" (4:1). The fact that he was a prisoner qualified him to exhort his readers. Today exhortation has gone out of fashion. It sounds arrogant to some people, especially to those who are unwilling to be bound by the absolute truth found in the Scriptures.

Even evangelicals are embarrassed by the memory of the exhortation of their fundamentalist forefathers who spoke with authority but did so in a way that proved to be unhelpful. So there has been a shift in proclamational style in many quarters of the church. It seems that entertainment has replaced passion as a means of attracting people to the church.

Sadly, we blew it by letting passion become an art form without the foundation of sincerity. We permitted powerful preachers whose lives were not holy and who were getting rich from preaching rather than suffering for the gospel to rise to the position of being prominent public representatives of Christianity. Charlatans have faked passion. Adolf Hitler misled a whole nation through his passionate speeches and led them to do things they would not have otherwise dreamed of doing. Naturally people are suspicious of passion today. Some see it just as a marketing tool used to good effect by people such as used car salesmen.

But burning passion is a characteristic of biblical preaching (Jer. 20:9; John 5:35; 1 Cor. 9:16). How can we restore it? How can we bring exhortation back into the church? One key is to have preachers who have been ignited by the truth of the Word through the Holy Spirit and are willing to pay the price of commitment to that truth. The English word *passion* comes from *passio*, the Latin word for suffering.

When a Japanese youth, Toyohiko Kagawa (1888–1960), read the story of the crucifixion for the first time, he was overwhelmed with emotion. He asked, "Is it true that cruel men persecuted and whipped and spat upon this man Jesus?" He was told, "Yes, it is true." Then he asked, "And is it true that Jesus when dying on the cross forgave them?" "Yes, it is true," was the answer he received. Kagawa then said, "O God, make me like Christ." He became a Christian, and that became his life's prayer.

Kagawa was disowned by his family, but he remained steadfast in his faith. He enrolled in a theological seminary, and while he was there he came down with tuberculosis and nearly died of it. He saw the poverty, exploitation, and prostitution in the city and was appalled. Though he was in bad health, he went to live in the slums. There he toiled on behalf of the poor for fifteen years. Kagawa became a famous evangelist and social reformer.

While he was on a trip to the USA he spoke at a meeting, and someone who heard him said to another, "Well, he didn't say much, did he?" The other person replied, "No he didn't say much, but if you're hanging on a cross, you don't have to say much."[2]

A cynicism is growing within the church. Christians have seen too many leaders fail to live up to their profession. They have seen selfishness when the agenda to which the leader asked the people to commit themselves turned out to be more a personal agenda than a kingdom agenda. They have seen leaders using the church to get rich, sometimes by exploiting weak and vulnerable people. They have seen preachers who do not practice what they preach. They have seen leaders who call for commitment to a mission and then exploit and misuse those who are thus committed.

If this trend goes on, we could end up with a dark age in the church. If the leaders who proclaim the truth do not live the truth, Christians could end up rejecting the message they preached. How can we bring back a healthy respect for the truth in the church? One way is to proclaim the truth wisely under the anointing of the Spirit. Another way is for leaders to faithfully live the Christian life and pay the price for doing so. We need leaders who are willing to give up comfort, convenience, and even a good name for the sake of truth. We need leaders who while suffering for the truth still maintain the joy of the Lord and thus testify to the greatness of the gospel they preach. Then people will conclude that if suffering does not take away our joy, the life of obedience to God is indeed the best way to live.

Perhaps someone reading this is presently suffering for the truth and is finding that very difficult to bear. You are hurting, and even worse, you are humiliated because people are feeling sorry for you. You experience much inconvenience because of what you believe to be the cause of Christ. Do not give up! "Let us not grow weary of doing good, for in due season we will reap, if we do not give up" (Gal. 6:9). Not only will we reap a harvest, we will also help influence the attitude of the church toward its leadership. We will help Christians believe there are leaders who are people of integrity. That will help create a new quest for personal integrity in the church.

Chapter Nineteen

COMMITMENT BEGETS COMMITMENT

I n our ministry with Youth for Christ we work primarily through volunteers. Over the years we have found that capable volunteers will not stay committed to the program if their leaders do not work hard and pay the price of commitment to it. But when volunteers see their leaders committed passionately to the program and its people going through hardship because of that commitment, they are spurred on to pay the price themselves. The commitment of leaders begets commitment among the members.

There is a crisis of commitment in the church today. It is difficult to get people to devote time and energy at personal cost to help the church thrive. Some churches have a large paid staff that focuses on providing services to prospective members. This is a marketing strategy that helps numerical growth. So people go to a given church because they have a good children's or youth program or because of the quality of music at worship services. The problem is that many will come to the church as consumers of the services that the church offers rather than as servants of the church.

In the biblical model the suffering of the leaders encourages commitment among the members. Paul tells the Christians in Philippi that his imprisonment "has really served to advance the gospel" (Phil. 1:12). Paul explains by saying that "the whole imperial guard and . . . all the rest" have come to know "that my imprisonment is for Christ" (v. 13). This had a positive effect on the church in (probably) Rome: "And most of the brothers, having become confident in the Lord by my imprisonment, are much more bold to speak the word without fear" (v. 14). Paul's boldness in prison encouraged the other Christians to be bold.

Paul even told the Ephesians that his sufferings for them were their glory: "So I ask you not to lose heart over what I am suffering for you, which is your glory" (Eph. 3:13). When our leaders suffer for us, that lifts us up to glorious heights.

Jesus explains the glory of this kind of suffering by contrasting himself as the Good Shepherd with the hired hand who runs away when the sheep are in danger. The Good Shepherd, on the other hand, dies for the sheep (John 10:11-15). Many people today come to our churches after bitter experiences of disappointment over being abandoned by people they trusted when they needed them most. Those who failed them could be parents or other family members, teachers, colleagues, or church leaders. Because of their hurts they may find it difficult to even trust God to truly care for them. What a breath of fresh air it will be for them to see a leader who is truly committed to them and who suffers inconvenience, tiredness, financial loss, or some other loss in order to help them.

Many recipients of such commitment by leaders in turn respond with commitment to the program the leaders represent. If the leaders die, literally or figuratively, for the people, the people will die for the church. Today we often hear Christian leaders bemoaning the lack of commitment among their people. They try organizing various training programs to help foster the increase in the number and quality of members committed to the programs of the church. These programs may be helpful. But I believe that the key lies in the love that the leaders have for these people. Their commitment will beget the commitment of the people.

I once had the difficult challenge of winning the confidence of a colleague I had been asked to supervise. His previous supervisor, with whom he had been very close, had left our staff. This had been a great source of disappointment to the colleague I am talking about. I saw that this colleague lacked any motivation to do his job, and we were at a loss to know what to do. We even wondered if we should ask him to leave. However, with time his attitude changed, and today he is a trusted colleague who has sacrificed much for the ministry. He is also one of my dearest friends, and he has often ministered God's grace to me.

Some years after his attitude had changed for the better, he told me that a key factor in that process of change was what happened the day his father-in-law died. At that time his relationship with our organization was not good. But he informed me of the death the moment his father-in-law passed away. I immediately went to the house.

I found that because the person had died at home, there were a lot of complications in the process of getting his death certificate. Because of my age and some other factors, my working on it was a decided advantage to the family. I had a heavy load of work to do at that time. But I spent the whole morning going from place to place with my colleague, meeting several officials until we were able to get the certificate. My colleague told me that what I did that morning was a decisive factor in triggering a process of change in his attitude toward me.

Today many churches are following a corporate model of operation with a heavy emphasis being laid on the program and the goals of the church. The leaders' job descriptions have become task-oriented rather than nurture-oriented. The title of a recent book by Glenn Wagner on this problem highlights the crisis before us: *Escape from Church, Inc.: The Return of the Pastor-Shepherd.*[1]

The idea of a leader caring for, teaching, and nurturing a few people is going out of fashion. It seems to be too cumbersome a task in this era of specialization. Preachers don't want to go through the frustration of spending long hours visiting those under their care and helping out with their problems—there are experts to do such things. After all, we have professional counselors and other experts to help people with their troubles and needs. Pastors of visitation look after the pastoral visitation. Preachers focus on preaching.

Yet this model does little to foster true commitment. Because the focus is on programs and services offered to the consumer, people will change churches according to what a church has to offer them. They joined a given church because it offered certain things. But when they sense that what they need at a new stage in their life is better provided by another church, they will change to that church.

Actually when extreme specialization takes place, the proclamation of the church will lack penetrative insight that will truly help effect change in people. Good preaching requires careful study of the Word and the world. That is something that specialist preachers can do well. But it also requires firsthand experience of the frustration and reward, the joy and pain of working with people. Without that, messages may reach high levels of technical excellence but will be low on potent insight. Great Christian leaders like Augustine, Luther, Calvin, and Wesley, whose preaching and writing had such a huge impact on the history of the church, all also spent great amounts of time ministering to individuals.

Biblical leaders are shepherds who love their sheep and are willing to die for them. And their commitment will foster commitment in the people they lead.

Chapter Twenty

AVOID COMMITMENT AND AVERT SUFFERING

S ri Lanka has faced a lot of pain in the past twenty-five years. We've had a war in the north and east, a revolution in the south, a devastating tsunami, several floods and epidemics, and persecution of Christians doing evangelism. Sometimes my friends abroad mention how fortunate they are that they do not have to live with so much pain. Indeed they are fortunate, but if I am able, I tell them that my greatest pain over the past twenty-five years has not been from any of these tragedies that struck Sri Lanka. Indeed there has been fear, frustration, sorrow, and anxiety. But the greatest pain has been from relationships. It is the pain that comes from being committed to people. And Christians will face that wherever they live.

Paul shared long lists of his sufferings in his epistles. But it is clear from the tone of different passages that his greatest pain came through the sin, wrong beliefs, and rejection of the Christians in the churches he helped found. In fact, his lists of sufferings were mostly given as pleas to his readers to accept his credibility without rejecting him and what he taught, given how much he had suffered for the gospel.

Whatever nation or culture we live in, if we are committed to people, we will face much pain. When Paul faced rejection and pain from the churches, he did not give up on them and go on with the ministry God had given him. He grappled with them through his letters. Most of these letters were sent to churches he or his colleagues had founded. As the believers were his children, it is understandable that Paul did not give up on them when they opposed him.

But trouble also came from the church in Jerusalem, which was not even responsible for his conversion. When people from Jerusalem tried to get the church in Antioch to insist on circumcision, Paul did not ignore it and go his own way with the Christians in Antioch with whom he and Barnabas had a close tie. The pair immediately made the long and tedious walk of at least four hundred miles to Jerusalem to deal with the issue. The result was one of the most significant theological developments in the history of the church, which helped release the church from ethnic Judaism and opened it to becoming a world community (Acts 15).

Our generation could be called the aspirin generation because people have become used to numbing and avoiding pain. This attitude has infiltrated our approach to ministry also. A common way this expresses itself is in Christians not being too committed to the group to which they belong and not getting too close to the people in the group. If we keep a safe distance from people, we can avoid a lot of pain.

In fact we are being taught to keep our relationships at a manageable level. There is some truth here. We can get so emotionally involved in other people's lives that their problems cripple us. However, true commitment involves investing in people so much that we become vulnerable to being hurt by them.

Our culture can also be called a throwaway culture. We are used to disposing of things that are not useful to us. Repairing broken things is too costly, so we just throw them away. Once while I was traveling in the West I was preparing a talk on the inevitability of stress in ministry. During that time three people told me how they or someone close to them liberated themselves from stressful situations. One person left a church where there was a difficult situation, and another left a Christian organization. The third person left her spouse and was liberated from a painful marriage. Each time I could not help asking myself whether it was God's will for them to stay rather than leaving the church, the organization, or the spouse.

Now I must say that there is some stress in Christian service that is unnecessary and that we must learn the discipline of maintaining our joy in the Lord even when things get difficult in ministry. And indeed there are some situations we must leave, believing that God has plans for us to be involved elsewhere. Sometimes this leaving is accompanied by a lot of pain, especially initially. Even Paul and Barnabas split after several years of fruitful partnership. And though they apparently had a warm relationship of comradeship later on (1 Cor. 9:6), the split was an unpleasant one (Acts 15:36-41).

Paul described the stress of commitment in this way: "And, apart from other things, there is the daily pressure on me of my anxiety for all the churches. Who is weak, and I am not weak? Who is made to fall, and I am not indignant?" (2 Cor. 11:28-29). Paul adopted an open-hearted approach to ministry that left him quite vulnerable to hurt. We can sense his pain as he told the Corinthians, "We have spoken freely to you, Corinthians; our heart is wide open. You are not restricted by us, but you are restricted in your own affections. In return (I speak as to children) widen your hearts also" (2 Cor. 6:11-13). We also see this vulnerability when Paul told the Galatians, ". . . my little children, for whom I am again in the anguish of childbirth until Christ is formed in you! I wish I could be present with you now and change my tone, for I am perplexed about you" (Gal. 4:19-20).

Here are some ways we can avoid the pain that comes with commitment:

- When members commit serious sins, we just let them leave us without going through the tedious and painful process of disciplining, healing, and restoration.
- When we have trouble with the group where we are involved, we leave and join another group without confronting the issues and persevering until a resolution is reached.
- When people question the direction we are taking, we can encourage them to leave and go to a place where they are more comfortable without going through the painful process of grappling seriously with their objections.
- When we are hurt or upset by something done by another person, we let it pass without confronting the person and working for a resolution.
- When someone in our small group has a serious problem, we tell them that we cannot help them because we don't have the time, energy, or resources to do it. (Sometimes we should not help some people for their own good. But usually we will help them, and such help could be really costly, resulting in exhaustion or depletion of our personal resources.)
- When people leave us unpleasantly, we let them leave without giving them an opportunity to talk about their grievances. (I believe exit interviews are very important when a person leaves unhappily. If that person is able to express his or her anger, there is a greater chance of that person putting the pain behind and starting afresh in the new place. If this is not done, they will carry an unnecessary burden for a long time that could stunt their growth into health after the pain. It is difficult for leaders to listen to the expression of anger by the person leaving. But that person is the one who is most vulnerable as he or she has to find a new place. Listening to the anger is the least we can do to help that person reconstruct his or her life after the painful separation.)
- Our call in Youth for Christ Sri Lanka is to go to unchurched youth. But present attitudes and possible anti-conversion legislation are going to make this very difficult as evangelizing youth is considered an unethical preying upon vulnerable minds. It would be easy for us to shift our focus to training Christians in youth evangelism. In addition to being a safer way of doing ministry, this would make us more visible to the Christians and would result in more funding for our work. But we must stick to our commitment to unreached youth.

When many Christians think of the cross they have to bear, they talk only about things like the persecution, unpopularity, and discrimination they face because of their principles. They do not include things that come from being committed to people, such as the exhaustion of helping them when we are busy and the pain of continuing to love them when they hurt us.

Commitment to people will cause pain to Christians of all nations and cultures. Of course, this meditation would be incomplete if I did not say that the joy of the Lord that is greater than the pain is what gives us the strength to bear the pain. We will see in the next meditation that commitment yields not only pain but also joy.

Chapter Twenty-One

COMMITMENT AND THE JOYOUS LIFE

I have worked for Youth for Christ (YFC) full-time for thirty-one years, and before that I was part of that family as a volunteer for another ten years. I can say that the greatest pain in my life has come from YFC. But I can also say that some of the greatest joys in my life have come from YFC. The greatest joys, of course, have come from my relationship with God and then with my wife and children. But YFC comes way up there as a source of great joy!

Earlier I mentioned an experience of speaking at a conference when the first talk in the morning did not go well. I was to speak again the next morning, and I went to my room very troubled. I talked to my wife over the phone and asked her to get people to pray while I struggled with the Lord into the night. That night I got a strange SMS text message about prayer from a young YFC staff worker for whose pastoral care I am responsible. When I went home, that colleague told me that he woke up in the middle of the night with a deep burden to pray for me. He felt I was in trouble—he thought I was facing severe sexual temptation—and so he earnestly prayed for me.

My talk the next morning went well. But what brings me most joy about it was that a beloved colleague got up during the night to pray for me. Such joys more than compensate for the pain of commitment. Painful situations sometimes linger for a long time. But commitment causes us to persevere without giving up. I have written my letter of resignation on paper a few times and many more times in my mind. But I never had the freedom to present the letter because I could not get away from the fact that God had called me to stay with this group and that I must stay on until I know clearly that it is God's will that I leave.

Incidentally, this year one of the hardest aspects of my pain through YFC has been that the challenges have been so great that I did not have enough time for the study I needed to do as a Bible teacher. The study I did was also done at some cost amidst severe exhaustion. But I know that prayer is the greatest way to prepare for Bible teaching. The story I just related shows that YFC gave me the great gift of praying for me, even though I had to struggle to find time for the other aspect of preparation—study.

To me 2 Corinthians has the most excitingly enthusiastic statement about the glory of Christian ministry in print. But the background to Paul's expressions of the sheer joy of ministry is one of severe pain. Paul hurt deeply over the rejection he faced in Corinth. His eagerness to know how the people responded to a letter he sent them is expressed in his impatience to see Titus, who took the letter to Corinth. This is how he describes it: "When I came to Troas to preach the gospel of Christ, even though a door was opened for me in the Lord, my spirit was not at rest because I did not find my brother Titus there. So I took leave of them and went on to Macedonia" (2 Cor. 2:12-13).

Yes, Titus did come with good news. But Paul did not mention that here; he just burst into a reflection on the glory of ministry. This is how he began: "But thanks be to God, who in Christ always leads us in triumphal procession, and through us spreads the fragrance of the knowledge of him everywhere. For we are the aroma of Christ to God among those who are being saved and among those who are perishing" (2 Cor. 2:14-15). This reflection goes from 2:14 to 7:1. In 7:2-5 he mentioned his love for the Corinthians and the joy that it brought along with the pain:

> *Make room in your hearts for us. We have wronged no one, we have corrupted no one, we have taken advantage of no one. I do not say this to condemn you, for I said before that you are in our hearts, to die together and to live together. I am acting with great boldness toward you; I have great pride in you; I am filled with comfort. In all our affliction, I am overflowing with joy. For even when we came into Macedonia, our bodies had no rest, but we were afflicted at every turn—fighting without and fear within.*

Only after all of this do we find the answer to Paul's questions about what news Titus brought regarding the response of the Corinthians to his letter: "But God, who comforts the downcast, comforted us by the coming of Titus, and not only by his coming but also by the comfort with which he was comforted by you, as he told us of your longing, your mourning, your zeal for me, so that I rejoiced still more" (vv. 6-7).

Second Corinthians is a good example of the deep joy that comes to us when we are deeply committed to people. Yes, there is deep pain too. But the joy compensates for that. And those who do not have the joy of deep commitment are impoverished as they miss one of life's greatest pleasures.

This is the joy of marriage—knowing that we love our spouses in spite of all the things about them that annoy us. There is a security, a sense of being loved, a freedom to give ourselves fully emotionally and physically and sexually to this person to whom we are committed for life. This is why lifelong commitment is a key to a truly happy sex life.

H. Norman Wright, in his book *Premarital Counseling*, talks about a couple who came for premarital counseling one day, and the young lady was really happy. He asked her why she was so happy. She said that about three days earlier her fiancé behaved in a miserable way. He was stubborn, obstinate, out of sorts. He was really a rat. But, she said, in spite of all that she had the firm conviction that she really loved him. She said, "That was so affirming to me to realize that even at the times when he might be very disagreeable and I might not really like everything he was doing, I'd still have this conviction of love."[1] That brought her great joy.

Recently I received an e-mail about a man who went daily to have breakfast with his wife who was in a nursing home with Alzheimer's disease. One day he had a doctor's appointment in the morning. The doctor sensed that he was in a bit of a hurry and asked the old man about that. When the man said he needed to go to have breakfast with his wife, the doctor said they should hurry up and finish the appointment. The man said that it is okay to be late since his wife had not recognized him for five years. The doctor asked, "You still go every morning even though she doesn't know who you are?" The old man smiled and said, "She doesn't know me, but I still know who she is!"

There is something beautiful about such commitment. Amidst the sorrow of a wife who cannot respond, there is the joy of loving her to the end.

The disposable relationships that characterize today's society have left people with so much insecurity. They are afraid to give themselves to relationships because of the fear that they will not last and breaking up will be unbearably painful. While we Christians too may have such fears, such fear will not paralyze us because we know that the most important relationship in our life is with the Good Shepherd who loved us enough to die for us. Yes, we too will face hired hands who run away when we need them. But we always have the love and care of the Good Shepherd of our souls.

With this security we can take the risk of committing ourselves to people and institutions. What a breath of fresh air that will be in a world of disposable relationships. It will help us restore the joy and security of commitment in today's world. It will also be a key to arresting the divorce epidemic that has hit our world. As we show people the glory of costly commitment and apply it to vocation, church life, and friendships, we can help bring back a culture of commitment among Christians. Once that is there, people will learn to apply it to marriage also.

Part Four

SERVANTS OF THE CHURCH

. . . the church, of which I became a minister according to the stewardship from God that was given to me for you, to make the word of God fully known, the mystery hidden for ages and generations but now revealed to his saints. To them God chose to make known how great among the Gentiles are the riches of the glory of this mystery, which is Christ in you, the hope of glory. Him we proclaim, warning everyone and teaching everyone with all wisdom, that we may present everyone mature in Christ. For this I toil, struggling with all his energy that he powerfully works within me.

COLOSSIANS 1:25-29

Chapter Twenty-Two

MINISTERS AND STEWARDS

I am writing this five days after returning from the large Urbana Student Missions Convention in the USA where I did four Bible expositions. The transition from being a speaker to being a leader is a difficult one. As a speaker I am like a celebrity exercising my teaching gift and doing the work I love to do. As a leader I am a servant of Youth for Christ for whom I work and a servant of my family. As a servant I must be devoted to serving them as best as I can. Their needs don't crop up based on my convenience. I have to fight to find time to study and write. In fact, this paragraph was written at 10:45 P.M. out of sheer determination to start this chapter before going to sleep, even though I am starting a day and a half later than I had planned.

As I said, the transition from speaker to leader was a difficult one. I was feeling rather discouraged about my inability to find time to study and write today. I decided to change my usual devotional study pattern, and I read for my devotions a book titled *Full Service: Moving from Self-Serve Christianity to Total Servanthood* by psychologist and pastor Siang-Yang Tan.[1] God spoke to me powerfully through that book. Dr. Tan describes how influenced the church has been by secular models of management and leadership, a lot of which is very helpful. But he says that one area where we differ markedly is in our understanding of greatness. In the Bible greatness is servanthood. To be great is to serve God and his people. Of course, my theology, explained in the first part of this book, also teaches me that what I now see as a trial will later prove to have produced something good. So I have no reason to be discouraged.

In our Colossians passage, after saying that he suffers for the church, Paul describes his relationship with the church in these words: ". . . of which I became a minister according to the stewardship from God that was given to me for you, to make the word of God fully known" (1:25). The Greek word the ESV translates as "minister" is *diakonos*, from which we get the English word *deacon*. The NIV renders it as "servant," which, I think, carries the sense more accurately. This word "generally [means] one who is busy with something in a manner that is of assistance to someone."[2] It came to have the meaning of "servant; helper, minister; deacon."[3] It was often used for one who serves at the table. Essentially Paul was using this word to say that he was devoted to the welfare of the church.

Elsewhere Paul uses an even stronger word, *doulos*, meaning "slave" or "bondservant," to describe his devotion to the church. He says, "For what we proclaim is not ourselves, but Jesus Christ as Lord, with ourselves as your servants [*doulous*] for Jesus' sake" (2 Cor. 4:5). And, "For though I am free from all, I have made myself a servant [*edoulosa*, "I enslaved"] to all, that I might win more of them" (1 Cor. 9:19).

After describing himself as "a minister" of the church, Paul says that this ministry is done "according to the stewardship from God that was given to me for you" (Col. 1:25). The word translated "stewardship" (NIV: "commission") "indicated the responsibility, authority, and obligation given to a household slave."[4] This term not only reminds us of our servanthood but also presents this work "as both a high privilege and a sacred trust."[5]

We have sufficient evidence in the Bible to believe that all Christians have a particular call or stewardship entrusted to them by God. The work may be hard, but we are the specially commissioned messengers of the King of kings, or as Paul said, we are Christ's ambassadors (2 Cor. 5:20). This truth hit me with much force when I had to write a letter to the British ambassador over a problem I had with the dates of a visa I received for the United Kingdom. I addressed him as "Your Excellency." About that time I was preparing a message on the passage where Paul calls himself Christ's ambassador. I thought, *Here I am calling the ambassador of the Queen of England "Your Excellency." And I am an ambassador of the King of the Queen of England.* A thrilling thought indeed!

The particular task assigned to Paul is "to make the word of God fully known" (Col. 1:25). This is a great challenge in this postmodern era when people are not very enthusiastic about objective truth. It is outside the scope of this book to go into a discussion on that. Let me simply present the ninefold task with which we are confronted. This is a task that faces all those entrusted with the nurture of Christians—parents, Sunday schoolteachers, small group leaders, pastors. We must ensure that we communicate God's Word in a way that is—

1. accurate,
2. persuasive,
3. understandable,
4. relevant,
5. attractive,
6. memorable,
7. practical,
8. comprehensive,
9. under the anointing of the Holy Spirit.

So as ministers, slaves, and stewards, our privilege and ambition is to serve the people to whom God has called us. But we do so believing that God's best for these people will dovetail with what is best for us. We may not always think it is the best for us. I have found that I often have to change my personal plans and give up my personal preferences because of the needs of the people I serve. And yet years later I always see that in spite of what looked like a big sacrifice, this was the best for me too.

In my book *Jesus Driven Ministry* I explained what servanthood means to a husband, using Ephesians 5:25 ("Husbands, love your wives, as Christ loved the church and gave himself up for her"). I wrote:

> Most wives would say, "I really don't want my husband to die for me. Just ask him to talk to me! He comes home from work tired and in such a bad mood that he won't open his mouth. He even gets annoyed when I try to talk to him." That husband is physically tired and emotionally drained after a tough day at work, and the last thing he wants to do is to talk. But because he loves his wife, he dies to his inclination to remain silent and talks to her. To him at that time, talking is a kind of death![6]

Sadly, our lopsided teaching on gifts has resulted in a lot of overspecialization, especially in the West. As we said earlier, some people spend most of their time exercising their primary gifts. So an outstanding preacher may not spend much time visiting church members and caring for the leaders of his church. The result of such specialization is a high amount of quality output by this person. But the impact of this person may be less than hoped for. To impact people we need more than technical excellence. We need depth-producing frustration that comes out of an incarnational lifestyle lived among the people we serve. We should use our gifts out of a lifestyle of caring for people. We should do a little of a lot of things and also try to give time to work on our areas of giftedness.

This is true in other professions too. Today in the intelligence sphere a lot of information gathering takes place through research and electronic surveillance. But often the conclusions arrived at come without the benefit of being in close touch with people. The result could be some major strategic errors. Decisions are made without fully taking into account the cultural factors that affect the mood of a people. To know such, one needs to get close to the people.

Those who had a marked impact upon the history of the church were leaders who wrote out of active involvement in grassroots ministry. Augustine went into the pastorate against his will because it shattered his dream of a tranquil life of study, prayer, teaching, and writing. Martin Luther, John Calvin, Jonathan Edwards, and John Wesley were, like Paul, active in grassroots ministry.

I always knew Calvin was a brilliant scholar, but I was surprised when I read the following about him: "He robbed himself of sleep. His home was always open to anyone seeking advice. He was constantly in touch with all the affairs of church and state. He visited the sick and lackadaisical, and knew almost every citizen."[7] Calvin once wrote, "Since my arrival here I can only remember having been granted two hours in which no one had come and disturbed me."[8]

We have found that many people coming back to Sri Lanka after higher studies are not prepared for the frustration of being servants of a struggling people. They come looking for the best package. They are not ready to die; they are not prepared for the frustration they will surely encounter. Their understanding of fulfillment is a worldly one that looks at it in terms of how they can best use their abilities and talents rather than how they can best be servants of God and the people.

Some leave after a time. Others become consultants who share their expertise with people without applying it through incarnational involvement with a group of people. Still others start their own organization where they can fashion their job description according to their own wishes. They all miss out on having a deep impact upon the people.

There is no escape. We cannot be effective in service unless we are willing to be servants.

Chapter Twenty-Three

SERVANTHOOD SPRINGS FROM GRACE

While most people recognize the value of servanthood, we also know that many who are recognized as exemplifying servanthood are very unhappy about their role. They work hard, but they are angry inside. They seem to be very humble, but sometimes their real inner feelings surface and are expressed like an explosion of anger. I believe the major reason for this is that their servanthood does not spring from grace. Let me describe three graceless expressions of servanthood and explain how grace can help us avoid such attitudes.

RESENTMENT

Many who are active in serving others struggle with resentment because they feel they have been exploited. They work very hard but get no recognition. People seem to take them for granted. Prominent people go on with their busy lives, using these faithful workers without recognizing their great contribution though they serve in the background. They sometimes scold them hurtfully if any obstacles appear along their prominent path. Those faithful servants then feel exploited and severely undervalued.

The first thing we must say is that faithful service behind the scenes is very important in God's sense of values, and if prominent people act as if they don't recognize that, these prominent people are wrong. Non-prominent work is difficult to do, especially in our media- and marketing-oriented society where appearance is so important. Those who don't appear in public could feel they are unimportant, and leaders must do everything to ensure they are properly recognized.

Yet, biblically speaking, all that we do for God is given to us to do because of his mercy (2 Cor. 4:1). We do not deserve the great honor of being servants in the work of the great God of heaven. Our lives are such that we are hopelessly unqualified for every responsibility we are given. Therefore everything is a bonus. When we realize that, we are grateful that God has chosen to use us, greatly reducing the disappointment of not being recognized. Such disappointment is natural because we are human. But when we address our disappointment with our knowledge that whatever we do is a bonus, we realize that we don't have a legitimate reason to be mad.

Speaking of his preaching ministry Paul said, "What then is my reward? That in my preaching I may present the gospel free of charge, so as not to make full use of my right in the gospel" (1 Cor. 9:18). The reward is the privilege of being able to preach without getting any other earthly reward. God's work is so great that just to be able to be involved in it, and without taking a salary (which is what Paul is saying here), is a great honor that we actually do not deserve. Robert Murray M'Cheyne quotes someone he calls Henry (Matthew Henry?) as saying, "I would beg six days, to be allowed to preach the seventh."[1]

All our service is an overflow of grace. The important thing is not what we do for God but what God has done for us. That is the key to the life of joy. We do well to constantly celebrate grace without looking to see whether our service has been recognized.

The elder brother of the prodigal son did not know this. He was angry about the grace shown to his returning brother. He complained to his father, "Look, these many years I have served you, and I never disobeyed your command, yet you never gave me a young goat, that I might celebrate with my friends" (Luke 15:29). "I have served you" (*douleuō*) literally means "I have slaved." Using the words of Paul, he had "the spirit of slavery" rather than "the Spirit of adoption as sons" (Rom. 8:15).

It will take us a lifetime to understand the glory of what it means to be adopted as sons and daughters of God. But as we realize it more and more, our joy increases more and more. We realize that God has been so good to us that instead of counting the cost of our service, our focus will be on rejoicing over the marvels of grace.

HURT

The next big reason for unhappy servants is the unkindness and insensitivity of people. When we are involved in any kind of work, we are going to be hurt. If the work involves pressure and people are tense, they are going to snap at us. Even worse than this is that others will use us to achieve their own goals and then discard us when we are not needed. Some will hurt us because of jealousy or annoyance. If we focus on the hurt that we have received after all our hard work, again we are going to become bitter and unhappy people.

But the Bible is very clear that "where sin increased, grace abounded all the more" (Rom 5:20). People may have been bad, but God's love to us is greater than all human wickedness. Paul says, "God's love has been poured into our hearts through the Holy Spirit who has been given to us" (Rom. 5:5). The word translated "poured" can convey the idea of a gushing out of the love of God in a flood. The most precious treasure in our life is this divine love, and it is greater than all the wickedness in the world. Therefore we must not give bad people the honor of taking away our joy. That is an honor they don't deserve.

Those who have tasted the joy of God, which comes through the overflow of his love, will battle for that joy when hurt. As we saw earlier, our battle with God may involve lament and groaning. But finally love shines through as God comforts us and we let his love be more influential in determining our attitudes than people's wickedness.

This is why it is so important to allow grace to heal emotions that have been damaged by people's actions. We may need help in facing up to the painful realities of people's actions. But we must persevere until we can say that God's love is healing us and is turning this evil into something good.

FATIGUE

One of the most common experiences of people with a servant spirit is fatigue. That in itself is not necessarily wrong, and we will discuss that in Chapter 28. We know that Jesus was often exhausted. But if we come to the point where we are drained so much that we have no energy left to serve others, the situation is serious and needs remedying. The key is to operate out of the love of God rather than out of our energy. "We love because he first loved us" (1 John 4:19). Talking about his ministry Paul says, ". . . the love of Christ controls us" (2 Cor. 5:14). This "verb implies the pressure which confines, restricts, as well as controls."[2] The love of Christ—that is, his grace in us—is what propels us in service.

Years ago I read a statement from a well-known British Baptist preacher, Francis W. Dixon, that I have never forgotten: "The hardest thing to do is the work of God in our own strength." Insecure people will never find fulfillment from their work. They will work and work and never be really happy because work in this fallen world cannot be a source of primary fulfillment. Such people become prime candidates for burnout. I believe that insecurity resulting in hard work and not hard work per se is the cause of burnout. My friend Susan Pearlman of Jews for Jesus once told a group of us, "Burnout takes place when the wick and not the oil is burning."

Another sad result of the hard work of insecure people is the phenomenon of getting too much fulfillment from a relationship with a person of the other gender who is not one's spouse. Because of all the hard work, the home is neglected, resulting in unhappy situations and rejection at home. Insecure people find rejection hard to bear. But in the office there is this other person who is so accepting and admiring, unlike the spouse. The person gets too much fulfillment from this person, and the result is an affair or an unhealthy emotional attachment.

So we must always ensure that there is a free flow of grace into our lives. Nothing helps this more than spending time with God. As we read his Word and pray, we have a wonderful sense of being undergirded by God. We realize that "the eternal God is [our] dwelling place, and underneath are the everlasting arms" (Deut. 33:27). Having experienced that security, we begin to thirst for it. And even when we miss our time with God, it hurts us so much that we long to have this time again, and we are not satisfied until that thirst is satisfied. The Psalms describe this thirst for God among the faithful (see, for example, Ps. 42:1; 63:1).

Last night I made a mistake with my alarm and had set it for the evening rather than the morning. I got up late and rushed for an appointment without having my devotions. In the evening I was able to spend an unhurried time with God. My wife also was praying at that time. She had had a very busy day. We both agreed that it was so refreshing to be in God's presence away from the distractions of our busy lives. I must confess that I was sorely tempted to be distracted. I had to shut off my mobile phone to battle the distraction! It is still true that "they who wait for the LORD shall renew their strength; they shall mount up with wings like eagles; they shall run and not be weary; they shall walk and not faint" (Isa. 40:31).

One of the most dangerous conditions a Christian can come

to is losing that thirst for being with God. I have seen this in some busy Christian leaders. Even when they have the time, they don't spend it with God. They have lost the taste of being with the Lord. They are too rushed in their approach to life to stop and be alone. They would rather spend their free time watching TV or doing some work. We can come out of such a condition through repentance and fresh commitment. But this must be regarded as a serious situation demanding urgent action.

It should not surprise us that many of the great Christians who served God and the church faithfully were also people of prayer. One thinks of Francis of Assisi, who was known to spend hours in the presence of God, sometimes only uttering the word "Jesus." While we may not agree with some of the theology of nuns like Mother Teresa, we know that their great service was backed by long hours of devotional exercises. Martin Luther is credited with the statement that if he had a lot of work on a given day, he spent extra time with God because he needed strength to do that work. John Wesley kept a punishing schedule but preached until he was in his late eighties. He also was known for his strict discipline of daily devotions. Toward the end of his life he said, "I am weary in the work, but not weary of it."

Let us make sure that all our service springs from grace.

Chapter Twenty-Four

WE ARE RICH!

Our last few meditations have majored a lot on the cost of servanthood. This meditation presents a rich blessing connected with gospel work. It is appropriate that we discuss this here because we should never present the cost of service without the underlying confidence that it is accompanied by joy and a reward that outstrips the cost.

MYSTERY

In Colossians 1:25 Paul describes his task as "to make the word of God fully known." Then he says something about this "word of God" that he proclaimed: ". . . the mystery hidden for ages and generations but now revealed to his saints" (1:26). We usually think of a mystery as something unknown or as something that can be found out through investigation, like in mystery novels. When the Greek word *mustērion* is used in the New Testament, it usually means "that which is hidden and undiscoverable by human means, but that which has been revealed by God."[1] In Ephesians 3:3 Paul writes, ". . . the mystery was made known to me by revelation." In addition to *mustērion* we find two other meaningful words here: *apokalupsis*, meaning "unveiling, revealing, revelation," and *gnōrizō*, meaning "to make known."

Clearly the gospel is a message that the world needed to hear and that God has now given to us through an unmistakable revelation of his mind. Religious pluralists say that the truth of each religion is discovered through human experience and searching. The above discussion would have shown that Christians view truth as something not discovered but disclosed by God. Peter puts it like this:

> *Concerning this salvation, the prophets who prophesied about the grace that was to be yours searched and inquired carefully. . . . It was revealed to them that they were serving not themselves but you, in the things that have now been announced to you through those who preached the good news to you by the Holy Spirit sent from heaven, things into which angels long to look.*
>
> 1 PET. 1:10-12

Evangelism is not easy in today's context. But we reach out with the strong conviction that this is the message of the Creator to his creation, and therefore it meets people's deepest needs and is their only hope. They may not recognize that fact, but we know it to be so and do all we can to help them recognize it. Even as they reject the message and persecute us, we know that this alone can fulfill the deep longings of their hearts.

The fact that what we proclaim is the truth of God helps me greatly when I am discouraged or tired and do not feel like preaching. Reluctantly I open my notes and go through them, and soon I am gripped by the fact that what I am going to proclaim is the truth. It is gloriously true and the only hope for the people I address. For a moment at least my discouragement and tiredness are forgotten, and I enthusiastically share the message with the people.

WEALTH

Paul goes on in Colossians 1 to describe the mystery further: "To them [that is, the saints, v. 26] God chose to make known how great among the Gentiles are the riches of the glory of this mystery, which is Christ in you, the hope of glory" (v. 27). There is a passing reference to the mystery of election here. "God chose to make known" to the saints this great "mystery." Why did he choose us? We will not know that this side of heaven. This is a glorious privilege that has been given to us. Of course, it is also an awesome responsibility.

Note how Paul refers to the "the riches of the glory of this mystery." The idea of the gospel being wealth appears five times in Ephesians and Colossians (Eph. 1:18; 3:8, 16; Col. 1:27; 2:2). David presents the Law as being even more precious than gold—the most precious metal: "More to be desired are they ["the rules of the LORD," v. 9] than gold, even much fine gold" (Ps. 19:10). People can lose the sense of the riches of grace as they get preoccupied with seeking things like physical health, earthly wealth, and success in career. Yet the gospel is more valuable than all of this because it fulfills the deepest longings of our hearts and has the most reliable and exciting plan for what happens after this life.

A tax assessor is said to have come to a home and asked the man of the house to list his possessions. This was his answer:

First, I have everlasting life.
Second, I have a mansion in heaven.
Third, I have peace that passes understanding.
Fourth, I have joy unspeakable.
Fifth, I have divine love that never fails.
Sixth, I have a faithful wife.
Seventh, I have healthy, happy, obedient children.
Eighth, I have loyal friends.
Ninth, I have songs in the night.
Tenth, I have a crown of life.

The assessor closed his book and said, "Sir, you are a very rich man, but your possessions are not subject to taxation."

We must not lose sight of the great wealth we have. Sometimes people deprive themselves of this true wealth in their quest for earthly wealth. They have no time to spend with God. Sometimes they disobey God's principles. They may succeed in their professions and climb to the top of the economic ladder, but they will not have those things that really bring them satisfaction. Jesus said, "For what will it profit a man if he gains the whole world and forfeits his soul? Or what shall a man give in return for his soul?" (Matt. 16:26). The greatest wealth is the gift of salvation and all that comes with it.

I have heard Christians say that God has not looked after them even though they were faithful to him. That attitude arises when we do not realize the riches of grace. God turned us around—we were headed for hell, and he has given us a place in heaven. And we say God has not looked after us! This is like people going on an uncomfortable ride to heaven complaining that they don't have some things that people on a comfortable ride to hell have. The ride is only for a short time. What matters most is where we end up at the end of our journey. If we lose sight of the great gospel truths that tell us what is most valuable in life, we can end up feeling deprived because we do not have earthly blessings such as health, comfort, wealth, and success.

Paul wanted the Romans to experience the depth of riches in Christ when he said, "May the God of hope fill you with all joy and peace in believing, so that by the power of the Holy Spirit you may abound in hope" (Rom. 15:13). The joy and peace come from believing. We must accept that God is good and will look after us. Then we can experience joy and peace. And even if things go really bad, we can still "abound in hope" and look forward to God's turning even bad situations into good ones.

After surveying the gospel and its relation to Israel, Paul exclaimed:

> Oh, the depth of the riches and wisdom and knowledge of God! How unsearchable are his judgments and how inscrutable his

ways! "For who has known the mind of the Lord, or who has been his counselor?" "Or who has given a gift to him that he might be repaid?" For from him and through him and to him are all things. To him be glory forever. Amen.

ROM. 11:33-36

After summarizing the circumstances of his salvation and his call to ministry, Paul burst out, "To the King of ages, immortal, invisible, the only God, be honor and glory forever and ever. Amen" (1 Tim. 1:17). May we too become accustomed to having our souls overflow with lofty praise as we think about our riches in Christ.

Chapter Twenty-Five

THE HOPE OF GLORY

In the last meditation we talked about how the gospel, which Paul calls a mystery that was revealed to us, is a great treasure that makes us rich people (Col. 1:26-27a). Immediately after stating that, Paul describes the content of the mystery: ". . . which is Christ in you, the hope of glory" (1:27b).

The expression "Christ in you" could mean that Christ is *among* the Christians or that Christ is *within* the believer. Or it could be a general statement including both ideas. Whatever the exact meaning, what Paul is saying is that the presence of Christ colors everything in our lives. Elsewhere Paul said, "For to me to live is Christ" (Phil. 1:21). We have looked at this idea, using different terms, in Part Two of this book.

An old man lived in what used to be called "a poor house." Poor houses were homes for poor elderly people. He was bent in two and obviously quite feeble. A visitor to that poor house remarked that it must be hard for him to live in there. He straightened himself and said, "I do not live in this poor house. I live in God." The presence of God in Christ colors all we do and brings brightness to our lives.

Paul explains that the presence of Christ with us is "the hope of glory" (Col. 1:27b). That is, the fact that Christ is with us assures us that we will one day experience the glorious fullness of our salvation.

Elsewhere Paul says that the Holy Spirit performs this function. The Holy Spirit "is the guarantee of our inheritance until we acquire possession of it" (Eph. 1:14). Using another metaphor he says, "We ourselves, who have the firstfruits of the Spirit, groan inwardly as we wait eagerly for adoption as sons, the redemption of our bodies" (Rom. 8:23). Both these verses are saying that the experience of the Holy Spirit with us is the assurance that we will experience the promised future glory. There is no contradiction here with our text as we experience the presence of Christ with us through the Holy Spirit. In fact, the Holy Spirit is sometimes referred to in the Bible as "the Spirit of Christ" (Rom. 8:9; Phil. 1:19; 1 Pet. 1:11).

So because we experience Jesus through the Holy Spirit in our daily life, we know we are going to enter into glory in heaven. E. Stanley Jones (1884–1973) was an American missionary to India who had a great impact on many intellectuals in Asia. In a book published when he was seventy-nine years old, he says, "Jesus Christ means to me eternal life. I don't get it hereafter, I have it now in Him. I am sure of heaven, for I'm sure of Him. To be in Him is to be in heaven wherever you are. So whether I live or die, so called, is a matter of comparative indifference."[1]

The main theme I want to leave with the reader through this meditation is that the prospect of heaven is a key to our joy, in fact to our whole life, here on earth. In our twelfth meditation on "Shame and Honor," we said that the doctrine of judgment takes away our bitterness. Now I am stating that one of the key aspects of the daily experience of Christ is that it assures us we are going to heaven. The Bible talks about heaven and hell often because a proper understanding of eternal destiny is a key to determining Christian behavior and attitudes. If we knew that this life is like a short journey that takes us to our permanent abode, our ambition would be to live in the present so that it would go well for us in our eternal home. The prospect of heaven helps determine our ambitions.

If we look at life here as a temporary abode, we won't be too upset by temporary setbacks. Neither will we be too upset when the wicked prosper by being wicked while our progress in society is hindered by our refusal to break biblical principles. The discomfort of the righteous is like the discomfort of a person who is going in an uncomfortable vehicle on a short ride to heaven. The wicked may be on the road to hell in a very comfortable vehicle, but that comfort does not change the terrible destination to which they are headed. Similarly we realize that costly service for others is not as costly as it seems at first because there is going to be a great reward for it in heaven. Jesus said, "Blessed are you when others revile you and persecute you and utter all kinds of evil against you falsely on my account. Rejoice and be glad, for your reward is great in heaven, for so they persecuted the prophets who were before you" (Matt. 5:11-12). The prospect of heaven gives us courage to follow Christ and also becomes a trigger for great joy.

The great hymn-writer Fanny Crosby (1820–1915—her official married name was Frances J. Van Alstyne) is a good example of what it means to have Christ in us as the hope of glory. When she was six weeks old, she had a slight cold that caused an inflammation in her eyes. The family doctor was out of town, and the doctor who treated her gave her the wrong medicine, which resulted in her becoming blind. She married a blind musician, and they had one child who died as an infant. She lived until she was ninety-five years old, and she wrote over eight thousand hymns. Her hymns were characterized by joy and emphasized praise, as evidenced by two of her most famous hymns, "To God be the Glory" and "Praise Him, Praise Him."

When she was in her fifties, her friend Phoebe Palmer Knapp composed a tune and brought it to her. Fanny said, "Play it for me." Mrs. Knapp played it, and she asked Fanny, "What does it say?" She turned and saw Fanny kneeling. So she played it again and then a third time. Fanny responded, "Blessed assurance, Jesus is mine." Shortly after that she handed over the completed lyrics of the beloved hymn to her astonished friend. It begins with the words:

Blessed assurance, Jesus is mine:
O what a foretaste of glory divine!
Heir of salvation, purchase of God,
Born of His Spirit, washed in His blood.

The first two lines reflect the statement that we are considering in this meditation: "Christ in you, the hope of glory."

One of her last hymns goes like this:

Some day the silver cord will break,
And I no more as now shall sing;
But oh, the joy when I wake
Within the palace of the King!
And I shall see him face to face,
And tell the story saved by grace;
And I shall see him face to face,
And tell the story saved by grace.

A minister once told her that it was too bad God did not give her the gift of sight. Her response was, "If I had been given a choice at birth, I would have asked to be blind. . . . For when I get to heaven, the first face I see will be the face of the one who died for me!"[2] Can you sense the joyous anticipation of heaven?

That should be so for every Christian. But for that to be so, we need to talk about heaven and hell and judgment. For preachers not to talk about it, and for parents not to tell their children about it, would be criminal negligence. If the Holy Spirit thinks this is a topic that needs to be mentioned often in the Bible, it must be a very important factor in helping us live the Christian life. In light of that, the scarcity of mention of this in the church is very strange.

The greatest thing about Christians is Jesus. And our experience of him is only a foretaste of the glory that awaits us. May those truths powerfully influence our approach to life. May they do so more than the sin and hypocrisy and corruption of the world. This is a theme that we will never be able to exhaust. The seeker is going to be treated to a lifetime of amazing discoveries. But all of this is only a shadow of the glory that awaits us and for which we await with eager anticipation. May those thoughts comfort us in our pain, motivate us to costly service, and be a constant reason for joy.

Chapter Twenty-Six

JESUS:
OUR MESSAGE

My father committed his life to Christ while he was a university student under the preaching of E. Stanley Jones (1884–1973), an American missionary to India. It was said of Jones that whatever subject he spoke on and wherever he started, he always ended with Jesus. If we asked Paul to summarize his message in one word, I think he would say, "Jesus." In fact, that is what he says after presenting Christ as the hope of glory in Colossians 1:27: "Him we proclaim, warning everyone and teaching everyone with all wisdom, that we may present everyone mature in Christ" (v. 28).

There are many urgent needs to which we need to pay attention. There are social needs, economic needs, moral needs, ecclesiastical needs, and spiritual needs. And faithful servants of Christ who want to represent Christ adequately need to address these issues in their own lives and in their ministries. They need to preach, teach, and advise Christians on these issues so that they may know how to respond in a Christian manner to the challenges they face in life.

Yet the key to everything is Jesus. He is the truth (John 14:6). As such, everything we do and think is judged according to the truth that is in Jesus. The great British missiologist and former missionary to India Bishop Lesslie Newbigin (1909–1998) said, "Jesus is for the believer the source from whom his understanding of the totality of experience is drawn and therefore the criterion by which all other ways of understanding are judged."[1] Therefore we must always focus primarily on Christ.

Charles Spurgeon (1834–1892) was arguably one of the greatest preachers of all time. Sixty-three volumes of his sermons are in print. He preached at the Metropolitan Tabernacle for over thirty years. In the first sermon preached at the newly constructed Tabernacle he said:

> I would propose that the subject of the ministry of this house, as long as this platform shall stand, shall be the person of Jesus Christ. I am never ashamed to avow myself a Calvinist, but if I am asked to say what is my creed, I think I must reply, "It is Jesus Christ." The body of divinity to which I would pin and bind myself forever, God helping me, is Jesus Christ, who is the sum and substance of the gospel, who is himself all theology, the incarnation of the very precious truth, the all-glorious personal embodiment of the way, the truth, and the life.[2]

More than thirty years later, these were the last words he spoke from the Metropolitan Tabernacle pulpit:

> He is the most magnanimous of captains. If there is anything gracious, generous, kind and tender, lavish, and superabundant in love, you always find it in him. These forty years and more I have served him, and I have nothing but love for him. His service is life, peace, joy. Oh, that you would enter it at once! God help you to enlist under the banner of Jesus even this day.[3]

Now perhaps you can see why this meditation is important in a book on joy and pain in the life of service. We will face much pain as we serve God. We will be disillusioned by our leaders. We will have sorrow, heartache, disappointment, frustration, and anger as we see those we invest in not living up to our expectations of them. We will find people misunderstanding or rejecting us despite our sincere efforts to be honest workers. We will find our work not recognized while that of others is. The complexities of church politics will first stun us and then produce a sour taste in our mouth as we ask, "How could Christian leaders act like this?"

All this can make us angry and bitter people. Then not only do we hurt ourselves, we also make the message we preach unattractive to those to whom we minister. We are thus destined to be failures in ministry.

Yet, though people disappoint us, Jesus never does. His grace is greater than all our sin (Rom. 5:20) and is sufficient for every challenge (2 Cor. 12:9). But not only does this grace minister to us, it is the only hope for success in ministry with the difficult people we have been called to disciple. Just a few hours ago my wife and I were talking about what a tough challenge it is to teach truthfulness and motivation to the people we work with who have come to Christ from backgrounds of extreme poverty. There will be many failures. But there is hope, for God's grace is greater than even these huge challenges.

Yes, we will need to study how to work with difficult people. We need to learn what the wisest and most effective strategies of service are. We need to address the issues that threaten to inhibit the growth of our people. We need to confront and condemn their besetting sins. But always at the background of our communication is the knowledge that Jesus is their only hope.

My pastor-theologian friend Peter Lewis of Nottingham, England, has written an excellent book, *The Glory of Christ*. In the introduction he reports a testimony of a preacher he heard while on vacation in Wales. The preacher said that when he was twelve years old he had a great hero, a sportsman who played rugby for his country and cricket for his county. The boy's bedroom walls were papered with newspaper cuttings about him and photos of him. Then in his fourteenth year he got to know the man personally. He used to go fishing with him, and he observed him from a different viewpoint. He "got to know the man and not merely the image."

Sadly for this young teenager, what he saw was not encouraging. The preacher said, "*And the nearer I got, the smaller he became.*" After some description of this, he changed his tone and said, "But God eventually led that downcast schoolboy to a new hero. And I have walked with my Jesus for thirty-five years now. In that time I have often disappointed him, but he has never disappointed me! I have got to know him better, *and the nearer I get the BIGGER he becomes!*"[4]

Yes, the life of service will bring pain with it. But Jesus remains wonderful. And he is our hero. So we have joy!

Chapter Twenty-Seven

DISCIPLES ARE MADE, NOT BORN

Talking about his evangelistic strategy, John Wesley once said, "I determined not to strike in one place where I could not follow the blow." That is, he would not preach the gospel anywhere without ensuring that there was an adequate means to help those who received salvation to become mature disciples of Christ. Paul would agree.

After saying that he proclaimed Christ, Paul went on to say how and why he did it: ". . . warning everyone and teaching everyone with all wisdom, that we may present everyone mature in Christ" (Col. 1:28). We are to warn everyone. That is, when people are in danger of doing wrong, we have to help them avoid it. And we are to teach everyone. That is, not only do we give them specific advice and instructions on the immediate issues they face—we teach them in such a way that they develop a Christian mind so they look at everything from a Christian viewpoint. In other words, we teach them what Paul called "the whole counsel of God" (Acts 20:27).

This work is to be done "with all wisdom." The word *wisdom* (*sophia*) "denotes the capacity to not only understand something (Acts 7:22) but also to act accordingly (Col. 1:9; 4:5). It is the latter which separates wisdom from knowledge."[1] So our warning and teaching must be done in a practical way. I am unhappy about the separation of the discipline of theology into dogmatic or systematic theology and practical theology. All theology should be practical. It should lead us to respond to what we learn in God-honoring action. That is why we say that theology must lead to doxology—the declaration of praise to God.

The warning and teaching is done with a goal in view: ". . . that we may present everyone mature in Christ." The word translated "mature," *telios,* "conveys a range of meanings: perfect, mature, complete."[2] The NIV opts for "perfect," and the NASB translates this "complete" and the ESV "mature." What we are talking about here is developing strong Christians who know the Word and live their lives accordingly.

The work of nurturing mature Christians in the church is well illustrated in the epistles of the New Testament, where there is a clear recognition that there are a lot of obstacles along the way and some Christians have stumbled over them. The verse we are expounding talks of warning and teaching, and all the epistles do this. The authors of the epistles explain the Christian way to handle certain tough issues, and they urge Christians to follow this way. Sometimes they command, sometimes they argue, sometimes they use sarcasm. They argue from the Old Testament, from common sense, from the teachings of Christ, and even from non-Christian writings. They call upon the church to discipline those who do not conform and rebuke them for their slowness to deal with sin in the body.

Paul was sometimes "gentle among [them], like a nursing mother taking care of her own children" (1 Thess. 2:7). He explained one aspect of this in the next verse: "So, being affectionately desirous of you, we were ready to share with you not only the gospel of God but also our own selves, because you had become very dear to us" (v. 8). That is, he surrendered his right to privacy so that he could truly open himself to them. He also said that he acted like a father: ". . . like a father with his children, we exhorted each one of you and encouraged you and charged you to walk in a manner worthy of God" (vv. 11-12).

But as we shall see in the next meditation, developing mature disciples is tough work. It is so tough that I believe the church is by and large neglecting it. People have become so market-oriented in everything they do that they want to have large numbers and project large expectations for growth without taking into account the fact that developing mature disciples is a cumbersome process with a lot of setbacks along the way. Today we find huge projected programs aimed at reaching millions of people through evangelism and discipleship. Wealthy entrepreneurs are impressed by the projects and give them financial backing. But I fear that these projected growth plans do not take into account the tough work of incarnational discipleship—where leaders become one with their spiritual children and walk through the growth process with them.

As the title of this chapter says, "Disciples Are Made, Not Born."[3] This title is from a classic book on disciple-making by Walter Henrichsen. Another classic book on the topic, by Leroy Eims, is entitled *The Lost Art of Disciple Making*.[4] It is an art we must recover.

I was once talking to a pastor working in an unreached area of Sri Lanka about the struggle to nurture godly believers among recent converts to Christianity. We talked about how important it is to explain the Christian lifestyle and to address areas of unholiness that we are seeing in the church. He said that most pastors today avoid doing that because it brings up many questions that are difficult to handle. People come to Christ because he meets their needs, not because they want to be holy. If we talk about particular issues of holiness, they are turned off and leave the church. So pastors avoid addressing these issues. If this is allowed to continue, we will soon have a highly nominal church.

Note that full maturity is not for just a few people. The goal is to "present *everyone* mature in Christ" (Col. 1:28, emphasis added). "Everyone" (literally, "every man," *panta anthropon*) appears three times in the Greek and in the ESV. In practice it may be that not everyone grows, as they should, to maturity. But that should not be the case. It is not excusable. We cannot rest until all are discipled to maturity. This is a problem with large churches unless there is a concerted attempt to ensure that everyone in the large church is in a small group. Otherwise it would be easy for people to come just as consumers. They get lost in the crowd as anonymous recipients of the programs offered by the church.

Numbers are important because they represent people who have come within the sound of the gospel. This is why Acts twice mentions the number of people who had joined the church (2:41; 4:4). But our focus should not be simply on numbers. We must ensure that everyone has an opportunity to grow. Each individual is important to God and thus to the local church also.

A minister, visiting a family in his congregation, noticed there were many children in the house. He asked the mother, "How many children do you have?" She began to count off on her fingers saying, "John, Mary, Lucy, David . . ." The minister interrupted, "I don't want their names—I just asked for the number." The mother responded, "They have names, not numbers."[5]

Everyone must be cared for, and we must not rest until that is done. As a church or Christian group grows, structures have to be set in place to ensure that individuals are not overlooked. If that is not done, even though the church may claim to have grown, it has not grown in the biblical sense. It has just become fat!

The verb used in Paul's description of the goal of disciple-making is significant. He says, ". . . that we may *present* everyone mature in Christ" (Col. 1:28, emphasis added). Several noted scholars, including F. F. Bruce and Peter O'Brien, have pointed out that

Paul is speaking here about the Second Coming of Christ. We are working toward a goal that will be realized only at the end of time. Our great joy will be to present the fruit of our labors to God at the judgment. On that day the people we invested in will be to us what Paul called the Philippians: "my joy and crown" (Phil. 4:1).

When my daughter was little, I used to take her to her preschool on my motorcycle each morning (motorcycles are the standard means of economical transport for middle-class people in Sri Lanka). I would often see a lady who brought about four little children to school in a van. They would get out of the van with her and then hold on to her, each one holding a finger as she led them to school. I often think this is the way I would like to go to heaven—taking along with me several people in whose lives I have invested.

Notice how often the prospect of future reward appears in Paul's writings. In just the previous verse he had talked about Christ in us being "the hope of glory" (Col. 1:27). The wonderful experience we have of Christ is but "a foretaste of glory divine" (from the hymn "Blessed Assurance"). Jesus also talked a lot about heaven and hell. In fact, his basic call to discipleship has several references to the last judgment. After talking about denying self, taking up the cross, and following Christ (Mark 8:34), he referred to the judgment in the next four verses. Mark 8:35 says that those who try to save their life will lose it, which implies eternal loss at the judgment. So does the talk of gaining the whole world and forfeiting one's life in verses 36-37. In verse 38 Christ explicitly talked of his return and the judgment given to those who were ashamed of him and those who were not. The prospects of heaven and hell are important motivations to accepting the offer of salvation, to growing in grace, and to the life of service.[6]

There is a medieval story of a man who in a dream saw a woman carrying a torch and a pitcher of water. The torch was to be used to burn the pleasures of heaven and the pitcher to quench the flames of hell.[7] The story teaches that by eliminating these supposedly unworthy motives for desiring heaven and fearing hell, people could begin to love God for God's own sake. But that is not what the Bible teaches. Heaven and hell are legitimate motivations for our devotion and obedience to God.

A short while ago I spoke to a group of ten Youth for Christ staff wives. We were talking about the cost of being in youth ministry and the heavenly reward for it. Our staff workers are paid reasonable salaries according to local standards, higher than in many Christian organizations. But if our staff worked in the business world or in one of the many international relief agencies that came to Sri Lanka after the tsunami, they would be paid much, much higher salaries. Even in Christian circles youth workers are not high up in the ecclesiastical status ladder. After working thirty years as a youth worker people still ask me when I am going to join the ministry!

One staff wife said that what some of her relatives say makes her feel ashamed and a failure in life. This is because her family does not have many of the things that are associated with affluence and success. I reminded her that the Bible talks often about the shame that we share with Christ and that it presents that shame in the light of the honor that will be given to us at the judgment. We discussed this in meditation #12.

I shared with that staff wife the analogy I've mentioned before of some going to hell in a comfortable vehicle while others go to heaven in a very uncomfortable vehicle. From the heavenly perspective, bringing eternal salvation to young people so that they have a whole life of service to God ahead of them is an extremely valuable work, even though the world does not regard it to be so.

If we knew the value of helping people prepare for their eternal home, we would consider the cost that we pay for doing this work well worth it. May the church bring heaven and hell back to the pulpit. And through that may she challenge many to follow the path of radical obedience to Christ and sacrificial service to humanity.

Chapter Twenty-Eight

TOIL IN
DISCIPLE-MAKING

I n his extremely helpful book *The Disciplines of a Godly Man,*
Kent Hughes says, "It has been said that the world has been
run by tired men, and it is true, for we daily see that America is
run by tired political leaders—and that wars are won by exhausted
generals—and that peace is secured by tired diplomats—and that
great legislation is accomplished by weary legislators." He says
that in the same way, "the Christian world is ministered to by tired
people. . . . Show me a great church and I'll show you some tired
people."[1]

Paul would agree. Immediately after describing the work of disciple-making, he says, "For this I toil, struggling with all his energy
that he powerfully works within me" (Col. 1:29). The verb translated "toil" (*kopiaō*) takes the meanings "work, work hard, labor
. . . become tired, grow weary."[2] Elsewhere Paul says, "For you
remember, brothers, our labor and toil: we worked night and day,

that we might not be a burden to any of you, while we proclaimed to you the gospel of God" (1 Thess. 2:9; see also 2 Cor. 11:27). Kent Hughes says that one day D. L. Moody's bedtime prayer was, "Lord, I'm tired! Amen." He says, "Luther is said to have worked so hard that he often fell into bed, not even taking time to change his sheets for a whole year!"[3]

Why does disciple-making require toil? I think the first thing we must say is that the balanced life, even without disciple-making, has so many facets that it can be tough on us. The balanced life for a Christian is not "everything in moderation" but "obedience in every area." So those seeking to live as balanced Christians must

- ensure that they have a vibrant devotional and worship life;
- meet regularly for fellowship with others who will spur them on to love and good works (Heb. 10:24-25);
- fulfill their family obligations;
- do their job and/or studies well;
- have contacts with the society around them, such as their neighbors;
- be informed of the world around them;
- have some fun time, preferably with family;
- take regular exercise.

Add to that the disciple-making ministry, and tiredness becomes inevitable. When we are working to ensure the complete maturity of a person, there are a lot of areas to work on. I have worked primarily with first-generation Christians most of my ministry life. Because they do not have a Christian background, many Christian values are not included in their way of looking at life. Their views of God and morality differ from ours. Many come with hurts and effects of abuse. So it will take a lot of work before they arrive at the completeness of Christian character. I believe this is increasingly becoming the case in the West too, as many who come to Christ know very little about Christianity and the Christian way of life.

In today's world disciple-making would include several activities:

- Regular personal appointments will help us minister to personal needs and help point to ways of dealing with issues they face in life.
- We must ensure that they are taught the basics of Christianity and also begin to feel at home with the Bible. Sometimes this can take place in a group setting.
- We need to visit them when they have special needs such as depression, discouragement, sickness, and backsliding. We may need to be with them at special days in their lives such as baptism, birthdays, and graduation.

I do not know of a better way to impart truth that is particularly relevant to their situation than being with people. Paul told the Ephesian elders, "You yourselves know . . . how I did not shrink from declaring to you anything that was profitable, and teaching you in public and from house to house. . . . Therefore be alert, remembering that for three years I did not cease night or day to admonish everyone with tears" (Acts 20:18, 20, 31). He was able to "admonish everyone with tears" because he got close to them. When we get close to people, we learn about the issues they face and then labor to see how we can apply biblical truth to their lives.

I think I too have been tired for most of my time in ministry. But I also think I feel as fresh and excited about ministry as when I started over thirty years ago. I believe one reason for that freshness and excitement is that I have had to study the Bible in order to give the people a fresh word from God for their particular situation. As one who has been given the task of helping nourish the flock, I have had to study a lot in order to teach them. Finding time to study amidst a busy ministry has been tough and has contributed to my tiredness. But the very thing that contributes to our tiredness also contributes to our freshness. When you spend time with the Bible, you are fed, you are convicted, you are thrilled, you are inspired, and you are fired up to proclaim it because it is God's Word. It is like charging a dead battery.

George Mueller (1805–1898) retired from directing the orphanages he set up and went into itinerant evangelism at the age of seventy. He traveled all over the world until he was eighty-seven years old. He lived into his nineties. When he was asked the secret of his long life, one of the three reasons he gave was, "the love he felt for the Scriptures and the constant recuperative power they exercised upon his whole being (Prov. 3:2, 8; 4:22)."[4] Tired but recuperated! Disciple-making forces you into the Word, and that in turn recuperates you!

Now I find that sometimes I am tired because I am doing something that I do not need to do. I find it very difficult to say no. This is aggravated by the fact that in our culture often *saying no* is taken as an insult. So I have had to get help from my board, my accountability group, and my wife in developing strict guidelines on what invitations I can accept and what I must not. This has helped me say no and has also given me some sort of protection from those who might accuse me of some unworthy reason for rejecting their invitation.

Another thing we must remember is to *divest* activities from our lives that we do not need to be doing. We must work with people to whom we are accountable and develop guidelines for what we should do and not do. My board has helped me decide that I should not generally serve on committees, as my work outside Youth for Christ and church should be in the area of teaching rather than being a committee person. I think the longer we stay in the life of service, the more we need to divest.

Then we must learn to *delegate*, as Moses learned from his father-in-law when he was getting crushed under the load of caring for the Israelites (Exod. 18). Good leaders don't need to personally care for everyone in the group they lead. But they need to ensure that everyone is being cared for. They need to enlist others to do some or even much of the work. Those who do things that others can do may be suffering from an unhealthy Messiah complex. They may be getting from their service the fulfillment that they should be getting only from God. Of course, a leader who consistently disciples people will find that volunteers emerge from the discipling ministry who can take on some of the workload.

Then, however busy we are, we need to *take a Sabbath*. That is done primarily as an act of obedience: if God said that this is good for us, it surely *is* good for us. Among other things, it refreshes us and helps us place the priority where it should be placed—on the God who works for us. When we stop working, we affirm that and learn to trust in God rather than in our abilities.

If we say no when we should, if we constantly divest, wisely delegate, and faithfully keep a Sabbath, why do we still get tired? I think one reason is that the needs of the people we care for often crop up at the most unexpected and inopportune times. Someone for whose nurture we are responsible may have an urgent need when we are struggling to get a sermon completed. We may need to see the person right away. If we do so, we cannot let our preparation slip. We must do the best job possible when proclaiming God's Word. So we may end up tired because in addition to the discipling activity we had to break rest in order to prepare our message.

I have taken family emergencies as something that I must absolutely be willing to sacrifice time to attend to. Our family members are our primary responsibility in life. So even though we are tired, we must care for them. I have tried to let my children know that however tired I am, I love to chauffeur them around if I need to. I think they have appreciated that.

Today is a Saturday, and I was very busy as, in addition to having some appointments, I needed to finish writing this meditation because of several deadlines. My son came home with two teenagers from the town where he is working as a schoolteacher and also serving as a volunteer YFC coordinator. He came to buy a drum set for the Youth for Christ band in his town. He needed someone to take him around. I volunteered to do that. The result is that tonight I will sleep much less than I had hoped to. But I am happy. And I think this approach to our children has helped both of them not to resent the ministry that took so much of my time and energy without giving much else in terms of earthly reward.

Let me say one more thing. Satan often tries to hit us hard when we are tired. And we need to know that. This is especially acute when we are tired because of a high-pressure event. In the letdown after the event, our adrenaline levels may be high, and we cannot sleep. We may also be dangerously vulnerable to temptation. I have read of pastors who visit prostitutes on Sunday evenings. We may be tempted to watch an unclean TV program in a hotel room when we return there after a heavy day of preaching.

The answer is to anticipate tiredness and arrange for wholesome things to do when we are tired. I usually request my hosts to put me in a home when I am preaching away from my home. In addition to being in a place with less temptation, chatting with hosts, though time-consuming, is a good way to get to know the audience I am addressing. I take clean mystery books to read when I am tired, as I usually am not in a mood to read Christian books at such a time. I take a radio along with me so I can listen to classical music (which is what I find most pleasurable) if there is a station nearby. And if I am staying in a hotel I will alert—through SMS text messaging—my accountability group and wife about where I am and about how I am faring there.

Chapter Twenty-Nine

HE GIVES THE STRENGTH

We have so far covered four aspects in Paul's description of disciple-making in Colossians 1:28-29: proclaiming, warning, teaching, and toil. Two more features are given in verse 29. We are involved in a struggle, but we are energized by God.

STRUGGLE

Paul says, "For this I toil, struggling with all his energy that he powerfully works within me" (1:29). The word translated "struggling" is the familiar word *agonizomai*, which appears eight times in the New Testament. John used it in a battle context when he used Jesus' words to Pilate, "If my kingdom were of this world, my servants would have been fighting [*agōnizonto*], that I might not be delivered over to the Jews" (John 18:36). Paul also used it in this way: "Fight [*agōnizomai*] the good fight of the faith" (1 Tim. 6:12a), and "I have fought [*agōnizomai*] the good fight"

(2 Tim. 4:7). Paul uses the word in an athletic context in 1 Corinthians 9:25: "Everyone who competes in the games exercises self-control in all things" (NASB). There "competes in the games" is the translation of *agōnizomenos*.

Disciple-making is a strenuous struggle for souls. Just this afternoon a young YFC volunteer told me, "It is such a struggle to disciple these fellows [teenagers]. They do YFC work and neglect their studies. They get involved in God's work and neglect their families. They go for days without having their devotions. Trying to keep them in line is so difficult."

In Paul's time and ours, the ministry of nurture is a battle for souls. There will often be disappointments. Paul faced that when the Galatians succumbed to false teaching. This is how he expressed his pain: "My little children, for whom I am again in the anguish of childbirth until Christ is formed in you! I wish I could be present with you now and change my tone, for I am perplexed about you" (Gal. 4:19-20). But that did not cause him to give up. It drove him to an even more concerted battle. So he sent them a letter that is now recognized as a masterpiece of theological argumentation. After the customary salutation (Gal. 1:1-5), he got right down to business by saying, "I am astonished that you are so quickly deserting him who called you in the grace of Christ and are turning to a different gospel" (v. 6). Most of the book of Galatians carries that tone of urgency.

Paul battled for the souls of the Corinthians just as he did for the Galatians. We see this in his description of how he wrote his so-called "severe" or "sorrowful" letter (which we do not have with us): "For I wrote to you out of much affliction and anguish of heart and with many tears, not to cause you pain but to let you know the abundant love that I have for you" (2 Cor. 2:4).

New Christians sometimes stray from God's way. The passionate, persevering commitment of disciple-makers is often what God uses to bring them back to his path. I have found that when our young people move away from the Lord, often the first one they start accusing is the very person who has done so much for their nurture. That hurts; but it is not sufficient grounds for giving up on them. There seem to have been Christians in Galatia and Corinth who said bad things about Paul. But he wrote to them the letters that made their way into the Bible.

The Scottish pastor Robert Murray M'Cheyne, preaching to his congregation, said, "I sometimes feel, brethren, that I would willingly lie down beneath the sod in the churchyard, and be forgotten and trampled on, if only you were friends of Christ."[1]

One use of *agōnizomai* by Paul is, I believe, pertinent to our discussion. In Colossians 4:12 Paul talked about how Epaphras was praying for the Colossians. Epaphras was originally from Colosse, and he may even have founded that church, but now he was with Paul. Paul said, "Epaphras, who is one of you, a servant of Christ Jesus, greets you, always struggling [*agonizomenos*] on your behalf in his prayers, that you may stand mature and fully assured in all the will of God." He was struggling in prayer from where he was, either Rome or Caesarea. I think this is where we get the expression *agonizing in prayer.*

When we intercede for someone, we are waging war on behalf of that person. This reminds us of the battle that Joshua led against the Amalekites, when victory was won through the prayers of Moses, with Aaron and Hur holding up his hands (Exod. 17:10-13). Paul continued by saying of Epaphras, "For I bear him witness that he has worked hard for you" (Col. 4:13). How could he be working hard for them when he was hundreds of miles away from them? By praying! When we pray for people, we are working on their behalf. I believe that is the most important work we do for the people we disciple.

Of course, while prayer is work, it is also a means of our being energized. When we pray, we are in intimate touch with God. The door is open for God's love to flood into us. But at the same time love is going out of us as we love people by praying for them. The result is that there is a free flow of love. Since God's love is bigger than our love, we can expect that more love comes into us than goes out of us. So love comes in, and love goes out! And in the process we are revived, energized.

In fact, I have found that praying for the people for whom I have a special responsibility is a good way to prepare to speak. I discovered this when I was preaching at the Amsterdam 2000 Conference for Itinerant Evangelists. I felt I needed anointing to speak to this large gathering. So the morning that I was to speak, I got up early in order to pray. After some time I felt I had covered all the petitions related to my speaking. So I took my prayer list and spent the rest of my prayer time praying for folks at home toward whom I had some responsibility.

Later I realized that my praying was a kind of preparation for speaking, for I was in touch with God and getting in tune with him through prayer. That is what I needed to do to open the door for the Spirit to flow through me. So though praying for others is a struggle, it is a struggle that energizes us.

We must note that some kinds of praying for others, like praying at church for those who come forward or praying to cast out a demon, can be very exhausting. After the woman with a discharge of blood touched Jesus and was healed, he said, "Someone touched me, for I perceive that power has gone out from me" (Luke 8:46). Power went out of Jesus when he healed this woman. In the same way special kinds of prayer can drain our spirits. But generally intercessory prayer refreshes us because it brings us into close touch with God. This brings us to our next point.

ENERGIZED

Paul said that he struggled "with all his energy that he powerfully works within me" (Col. 1:29). Paul uses three energy-related words to emphasize the point. A literal translation would be, "according to his working, which worketh in me mightily" (ASV). "Working" is a translation of the noun *energeia,* "worketh" is from the corresponding verb *energeō,* and "mightily" is the noun *dunamis.* Paul is leaving us with no doubt that all the energy for the work of disciple-making is from God.

As we stretch ourselves by toiling to see disciples of Christ grow into maturity, God gives us the energy we need to fulfill the task. Of course, we must follow the rules about which we have talked in the earlier meditations: learning to say no, divesting, delegating, keeping the Sabbath, and spending time with God. If we ensure that we use means that God has made available to us to be refreshed, then we can be sure there will be sufficient strength for the task. What God told Paul about his thorn in the flesh applies to the life of service also: "My grace is sufficient for you, for my power is made perfect in weakness" (2 Cor. 12:9).

- God gives *spiritual* strength by being with us and enabling us to do what we have to do. We go for an appointment with a wayward disciple of Christ, we pray for grace to speak to him in the correct way, and God gives us the words to speak.
- We sometimes feel very weak *physically* and unable to continue serving because we are tired. Suddenly an appointment is canceled or some such thing happens. And we are able to catch up on our rest.
- We sometimes feel *emotionally* weak because we got hurt through ministering to others. Now we do not feel like venturing out in service. God speaks to us in unmistakable terms when we read our Bible. We are encouraged and can go on. Or God speaks to us clearly through a message we hear in church, and we are encouraged to go on.

As Paul put it: "He who calls you is faithful; he will surely do it" (1 Thess. 5:24). In this section we have presented several promises that God will give us the ability to do what we need to do. May those promises strengthen us to serve God faithfully.

A Concluding Meditation

Chapter Thirty

A PARADOX OF THE CHRISTIAN LIFE

This book has placed before you one of the many paradoxes of Christianity. On the one hand, the Bible promises that God will look after the faithful and provide their every need. Jesus said, "But seek first the kingdom of God and his righteousness, and all these things [earthly necessities] will be added to you" (Matt. 6:33). Paul said, "And my God will supply every need of yours according to his riches in glory in Christ Jesus" (Phil. 4:19). David said, "I have been young, and now am old, yet I have not seen the righteous forsaken or his children begging for bread" (Ps. 37:25).

On the other hand we know that Jesus also promised suffering for those who follow him. Those words about God supplying our needs were written from prison. The paradox is seen in three statements that Jesus made about the suffering his disciples would encounter.

- After calling people to deny self and take up their cross of suffering, he said, "For whoever would save his life will lose it, but whoever loses his life for my sake and the gospel's will save it" (Mark 8:35). The suffering will yield real, abundant life.
- He said, "'A servant is not greater than his master.' If they persecuted me, they will also persecute you. If they kept my word, they will also keep yours" (John 15:20). Rejection and persecution will be accompanied by acceptance.
- He said, "I have said these things to you, that in me you may have peace. In the world you will have tribulation. But take heart; I have overcome the world" (John 16:33). We face tribulation with the confidence that Christ has already overcome the world. Therefore we have peace in the midst of it.

Similarly Paul writing to the Philippians from prison said, "I want you to know, brothers, that what has happened to me has really served to advance the gospel" (Phil. 1:12). So he was able to tell the Philippians, "Rejoice in the Lord always; again I will say, Rejoice" (Phil. 4:4) and to affirm that after they make their requests known to God, "the peace of God, which surpasses all understanding, will guard your hearts and your minds in Christ Jesus" (4:7). In the same letter Paul shows that knowing Christ is a treasure that is so great that it makes losing everything the world considers valuable insignificant: "Indeed, I count everything as loss because of the surpassing worth of knowing Christ Jesus my Lord. For his sake I have suffered the loss of all things and count them as rubbish, in order that I may gain Christ" (Phil. 3:8).

So for us suffering is not a big deal. The German Lutheran pastor Dietrich Bonhoeffer was one of the greatest minds in the church in the twentieth century. He strongly opposed the Nazi regime. When he was on a sabbatical in the USA, he was challenged to stay there and pursue his theological career rather than go back to Germany where it would be dangerous for him. He wrote to Reinhold Niebuhr, who had helped arrange the American sabbatical for him, saying, "It was a mistake for me to come to America. I have to live through this difficult period in our nation's history with Christians in Germany. I will have no right to participate in the reconstruction of Christian life in Germany after the war if I do not share the tribulations of this time with my people."[1] He was executed by the Nazis in 1945 after he spent two years in prison.

Bonhoeffer felt that people were making too big a deal over his suffering. About a year before he was executed, writing from the Tegel Prison to his friend Eberhard Bethge, who later became his biographer, he said, "There arises a protest in me when I read references in letters . . . to my 'suffering.' To me this seems like a sacrilege. These things must not be dramatized. It is more than questionable that I am 'suffering' more than you or even than most people today. Of course, much of what happens here [in prison] is disgusting, but where is that not the case? Maybe we used to take things too seriously and solemnly in this regard." Later in the same letter he says, "I must confess that I am sometimes ashamed at how much we have spoken about our own suffering."[2]

Of course, people will not understand. Some may admire our commitment, but many will think we are doing something wrong and despise us. Bonhoeffer talks of this in his book *The Cost of Discipleship*. Referring to Christ's statement that "the Son of Man must suffer many things and be rejected by the elders" (Mark 8:31), Bonhoeffer says, "Suffering and rejection are not the same thing." After describing how people could view suffering in a positive light, he says, "Jesus, however, is the Christ who is rejected in suffering. Rejection robs suffering of any dignity or honor. It is to be suffering void of honor."[3]

People close to us will try to get us to avoid the suffering. It is difficult to endure when fellow believers whom we love try to discourage us from taking the way of the cross. But we must remember that Jesus called Peter "Satan" (Mark 8:33) just after he had commended him for his strong statement of faith that Jesus was "the Christ, the Son of the living God" (Matt. 16:16-17; Mark 8:29). Commenting on this Bonhoeffer says, "Any attempt at thwarting the necessary is satanic."[4]

To survive along the way of the cross we need to develop a

biblical attitude toward suffering. Bonhoeffer is helpful again here. About a year prior to his arrest, he said in a letter, ". . . it is good to learn early that suffering and God are not contradictions, but rather a necessary unity. For me, the idea that it is really God who suffers has always been one of the most persuasive teachings of Christianity. I believe that God is closer to suffering than to happiness, and that finding God in this way brings peace and repose and a strong, courageous heart."[5]

Some Christians in the first few centuries of the church went to an extreme by desiring martyrdom. Nowhere are we told to go after suffering as if it is an end in itself. Those who are not suffering do not need to be guilty about that! Let them pursue total abandonment to Christ. Then, though they do not go after suffering, some sort of suffering will come because Jesus promised that. But when Jesus is everything to us, suffering is not a huge problem. If we have him with us, we have what matters most. His love for us gives us the joy that becomes our strength. Then we can bear suffering and remain totally fulfilled human beings in the midst of it.

I trust that this book has helped you develop an approach to life (or confirm an existing approach) that refuses to look upon suffering as a big deal. The big deal is always our relationship of love with God through Christ. If suffering helps us get closer to Jesus and be more effective in his service, then we will welcome it with joy, as Paul did.

Of course, all through our suffering we know that God will supply everything we need. Implied in that statement, of course, is the belief that God does not regard the absence of suffering as one of our basic needs.

As for Bonhoeffer, he died before he was forty years old, leaving behind his fiancée. Many people thought his death was the waste of a great resource for the church. But Bonhoeffer himself remained close to God and knew that his death would only bring him nearer to God.

Shortly before Bonhoeffer died he wrote a poem, "Stations on the Road to Freedom." He presented three stations. The first was "Action," "daring to do what is right." The second was "Suffering." And the third was "Death." He wrote, "Come now thou greatest of feasts on the journey to freedom eternal."[6] When he was being taken for what he knew was his execution, he told a fellow prisoner, a British soldier, to give a message to his friend, the British bishop George Bell: "Tell the Bishop that for me this is the end but also the beginning. With him [the Bishop] I believe . . . that our victory is certain."[7]

In terms of his theological contribution to the church, Bonhoeffer remains one of the most read Christians of the twentieth century. I think it would be correct to say that the popularity of his writings and the extent of his impact upon the church were influenced by the fact that he was martyred at the prime of his life. His sufferings certainly helped the church.

I will close this book by addressing both you and myself with Paul's words to his spiritual son Timothy: "Endure hardship with us like a good soldier of Christ Jesus" (2 Tim. 2:3, NIV).

NOTES

INTRODUCTION

1. E. Stanley Jones, *A Song of Ascents* (Nashville: Abingdon Press, 1968), p. 180.
2. I have attempted to do that briefly in *The Supremacy of Christ* (Wheaton, IL: Crossway Books, 1995; London: Hodder & Stoughton, 1997; Secunderabad, India: OM Books, 2005), Chapter 14, "The Cross and the Problem of Pain" and in *After the Tsunami* (U.S. edition: *After the Hurricane*), Discovery Booklets (Grand Rapids, MI: RBC Ministries). See also the forthcoming DVD provisionally titled *The God of Pain and the God of Joy*, Day of Discovery (Grand Rapids, MI: RBC Ministries, 2007).

CHAPTER ONE: TWO BASIC ASPECTS OF CHRISTIANITY

1. Paul Tournier, *Creative Suffering* (London: SCM Press, 1982), p. 60.
2. F. W. Bourne, *Billy Bray: The King's Son* (London: Epworth Press, 1937), p. 46.
3. Ibid., p. 23.

CHAPTER TWO: A FORGOTTEN TREASURE

1. This phrase come from David Augsburger, *Caring Enough to Confront: The Love-Fight* (Glendale, CA: Regal Books, 1973).
2. Etta Linnemann, *Historical Criticism of the Bible: Methodology or Ideology?* trans. Robert W. Yarbrough (Grand Rapids, MI: Baker Book House, 1990).
3. C. S. Lewis, *Reflections on the Psalms* (New York: Harcourt Brace and World Inc. 1958), p. 55.
4. Ibid., p. 62.
5. C. S. Lewis, *Surprised by Joy: The Shape of My Early Life* (New York: Harcourt Brace Jovanovich, 1960), p. 170.

CHAPTER THREE: BURSTS OF PLEASURE

1. A. J. Appasamy, *Sundar Singh: A Biography* (Madras: Christian Literature Society, 1966), p. 19.
2. See Steven Tracy, "Chastity and the Goodness of God: The Case for Premarital Sexual Abstinence," *Themelios*, Vol. 31, No. 2 (January 2006), pp. 54-71.

CHAPTER FOUR: LAMENT

1. *The New International Version Study Bible Notes*, Pradis CD-ROM: Lamentations.
2. J. Clinton McCann, *A Theological Introduction to the Book of Psalms: The Psalms as Torah* (Nashville: Abingdon Press, 1993), p. 85; quoted in Nancy J. Duff, "Recovering Lamentation as a Practice in the Church," in Sally A. Brown and Patrick D. Miller, eds., *Lament: Reclaiming Practices in Pulpit, Pew and Public Square* (Louisville: Westminster John Knox Press, 2005), p. 4.
3. Chris Wright, "Personal Struggle and the Word of Lament," in *Truth on Fire: Keswick Ministry 1998*, ed. David Porter (Carlisle, Cumbria, UK: OM Publishing, 1998), p. 29.

CHAPTER FIVE: FAITH AND ENDURANCE

1. Num. 14:8; Deut. 30:9; Ps. 37:23; 41:11; 147:11; 149:4; Isa. 62:4.
2. Deut. 28:63; 30:9; Mic. 7:18.
3. Ps. 35:27.

Notes

4. From Charles H. Spurgeon, *Spurgeon at His Best*, ed. Tom Carter (Grand Rapids, MI: Baker, 1988), pp. 323ff.
5. See, for example, Rom. 2:7; 5:3-4; 8:25; 15:4-5; Rev. 1:9; 2:2-3, 19; 3:10; 13:10; 14:12.
6. Leon Morris, *The Epistle to the Romans* (Grand Rapids, MI: Eerdmans; Leicester: Inter-Varsity Press, 1988), p. 325.
7. Paul Sangster, *Dr. Sangster* (London: Epworth Press, 1962), p. 54; cited in Warren W. Wiersbe and Lloyd M. Perry, *The Wycliffe Handbook of Preaching and Preachers* (Chicago: Moody Press, 1984), p. 217.
8. W. E. Sangster, *Westminster Sermons*, Vol. 2, *At Fast and Festival* (London: Epworth Press, 1961); from the Foreword by P. E. Sangster.
9. Martyn Lloyd-Jones, *Spiritual Depression* (Grand Rapids, MI: Eerdmans, 1965), p. 20.
10. Quoted in George E. Good, *Living Stones* (Newtownards, Northern Ireland: April Sky Design, 2004), p. 57.

CHAPTER SEVEN: NOT GLUTTONS FOR PUNISHMENT

1. Mrs. Arthur Parker, *Sadhu Sundar Singh: Called of God* (Madras: Christian Literature Society, 1918), pp. 25-26.
2. J. B. Lightfoot, *Epistle of St Paul to the Philippians* (Grand Rapids, MI: Zondervan; Pradis Electronic Version produced by Zondervan Interactive, 2004).
3. Cited in Dennis Kinlaw, *This Day with the Master* (Grand Rapids, MI: Zondervan, 2004), December 31.

CHAPTER EIGHT: A THEOLOGICAL BLIND SPOT?

1. A. T. Robertson, *The Glory of the Ministry: Paul's Exultation in Preaching* (Grand Rapids, MI: Baker, 1911, reprint 1979).

CHAPTER NINE: THE FELLOWSHIP OF SUFFERING

1. David E. Garland, *The NIV Application Commentary: Colossians and Philemon* (Grand Rapids, MI: Zondervan, 1998; Pradis Electronic Version produced by Zondervan Interactive, 2004).
2. Peter O'Brien, *Commentary on Philippians*, The New International Greek Testament Commentary (Grand Rapids, MI and Cambridge, UK: Eerdmans, 1991).
3. Cited in James S. Stewart, "Wearing the Thorns as a Crown," *Classic Sermons on Suffering*, comp. Warren W. Wiersbe (Grand Rapids, MI: Kregel, 1984), p. 92.
4. In Jan Pit, compiler, *Bound to Be Free: With the Suffering Church* (Tonbridge, UK: Sovereign World, 1995), p. 341.
5. In ibid., p. 142.
6. Cited in A. J. Appasamy, *Sundar Singh: A Biography* (Madras: Christian Literature Society, 1966), p. 27.
7. Ibid., p. 117.
8. Cited in Sherwood Elliot Wirt and Kersten Beckstrom, *Living Quotations for Christians* (New York: Harper & Row, 1974), p. 266.
9. Graham Kendrick, Make Way Music, 1993.

CHAPTER TEN: BECOMING LIKE CHRIST

1. I am grateful to colleagues from Youth for Christ in Trivandrum, India, who alerted me to this verse.
2. W. Arndt, F. W. Danker, and W. Bauer, *A Greek-English Lexicon of the New Testament and Other Early Christian Literature*, 3rd edition (Chicago: University of Chicago Press, 2000), p. 958.
3. Extracted from Mark Water, compiler, *The New Encyclopedia of Christian Martyrs* (Grand Rapids, MI: Baker, 2001), p. 856.

CHAPTER ELEVEN: MOTIVES PURIFIED

1. Dennis F. Kinlaw, *How to Have the Mind of Christ* (Nappanee, IN: Evangel Publishing House), pp. 72-73.

CHAPTER TWELVE: SHAME AND HONOR

1. I owe this insight to John Piper's book *The Purifying Power of Living by Faith in . . . Future Grace* (Sisters, OR: Multnomah Books, 1995), pp. 262-266.
2. I have heard many versions of this story, and the gist of what I have heard always has been the same, though the details have been different. So I have refrained from giving details.

CHAPTER THIRTEEN: SOLIDARITY WITH CHRIST

1. J. W. Mieklejohn, "David Livingstone," *New International Dictionary of the Christian Church* (Grand Rapids, MI: Zondervan, 2002; Pradis Electronic Version produced by Zondervan Interactive, 2004).
2. From Dennis Kinlaw, *This Day with the Master* (Grand Rapids, MI: Zondervan, 2004), March 2.
3. Kingsway's Thankyou Music, 1986.

CHAPTER FOURTEEN: SUFFERING AND CHURCH GROWTH

1. This information is gleaned from *A History of the Methodist Church in Ceylon* (Colombo: The Wesley Press, n.d.), pp. 23-28, 89-91, 658-659.
2. This story was related by my seminary teacher, Dr. John T. Seamands.

CHAPTER FIFTEEN: DEMONSTRATING THE GOSPEL

1. This version of the story is taken primarily from Mark Water, compiler, *The New Encyclopedia of Christian Martyrs* (Grand Rapids, MI: Baker, 2001), p. 431.
2. Rodney Stark, *The Rise of Christianity: How the Obscure, Marginal Jesus Movement Became the Dominant Religious Force in the Western World in a Few Centuries* (San Francisco: Harper San Francisco, 1997), pp. 73-94.
3. A. J. Broomhall, *Hudson Taylor and China's Open Century,* Book Seven: *1888-1988, It Is Not Death to Die* (London: Hodder and Stoughton and Overseas Missionary Fellowship, 1989), p. 32.
4. Ibid., pp. 480-481.

CHAPTER SIXTEEN: IDENTIFYING WITH PEOPLE

1. *Merriam Webster's Collegiate Dictionary*, electronic version.
2. Cited in Mark Water, compiler, *The New Encyclopedia of Christian Martyrs* (Grand Rapids, MI: Baker, 2001), p. 947.
3. This story is related in Dennis F. Kinlaw, *This Day with the Master* (Grand Rapids, MI: Zondervan, 2004), April 4. I got many details from a piece that Dr. Charles Killian of Asbury Theological Seminary had written. I am grateful to missionary anthropologist Dr. Darrell Whiteman who shared this with me.

CHAPTER SEVENTEEN: DEEPENING OUR IMPACT

1. Leon L. Morris, "Hebrews," *Expositor's Bible Commentary*, Frank E. Gaebelein, general editor (Grand Rapids, MI: Zondervan, 1976–1992; Pradis Electronic Version produced by Zondervan Interactive, 2004).
2. Ibid.
3. James S. Stewart, "Wearing the Thorns as a Crown," *Classic Sermons on Suffering*, comp. Warren W. Wiersbe (Grand Rapids, MI: Kregel, 1984), p. 92.
4. Dennis F. Kinlaw, *This Day with the Master* (Grand Rapids, MI: Zondervan, 2004), September 11.

CHAPTER EIGHTEEN: SUFFERING AND CREDIBILITY

1. James M. Boice, "Galatians," *Expositor's Bible Commentary*, Frank E Gaebelein, general editor (Grand Rapids, MI: Zondervan; Pradis Electronic Version produced by Zondervan Interactive, 2004).
2. From E. Stanley Jones, *The Word Became Flesh* (Nashville: Abingdon Press, 1963), p. 288.

CHAPTER NINETEEN: COMMITMENT BEGETS COMMITMENT

1. E. Glenn Wagner, *Escape from Church, Inc.: The Return of the Pastor-Shepherd* (Grand Rapids, MI: Zondervan, 1999).

CHAPTER TWENTY-ONE: COMMITMENT AND THE JOYOUS LIFE

1. H. Norman Wright, *Premarital Counseling* (Chicago: Moody Press, 1981), p. 99.

CHAPTER TWENTY-TWO: MINISTERS AND STEWARDS

1. Siang-Yang Tan, *Full Service: Moving from Self-Serve Christianity to Total Servanthood* (Grand Rapids, MI: Baker, 2006).
2. F. W. Danker, editor, *A Greek-English Lexicon of the New Testament and Other Early Christian Literature*, 3rd edition, based on the German lexicon by Walter Bauer and previous editions by W. F. Arndt, F. W. Gingrich, and F. W. Danker (Chicago: University of Chicago Press, 2000), p. 230.
3. Barclay Newman, *NT Greek-English Dictionary* (United Bible Societies, from the electronic version by WORDsearch 7).
4. Cleon L. Rogers Jr. and Cleon L. Rogers III, *New Linguistic & Exegetical Key to the Greek New Testament* (Grand Rapids, MI: Zondervan, 2003; Pradis Electronic Version produced by Zondervan Interactive, 2004).
5. Curtis Vaughn, "Colossians," *Expositor's Bible Commentary*, Frank E. Gaebelein, general editor (Grand Rapids, MI: Zondervan, Pradis Electronic Version produced by Zondervan Interactive, 2004).
6. Ajith Fernando, *Jesus Driven Ministry* (Wheaton, IL: Crossway Books, 2002), p. 185.
7. J. van Zyl, "John Calvin the Pastor," in *The Way Ahead*, quoted in Derek J. Tidball, *Skillful Shepherds: An Introduction to Pastoral Theology* (Grand Rapids, MI: Zondervan, 1986), p. 190.
8. Ibid., p. 73.

CHAPTER TWENTY-THREE: SERVANTHOOD SPRINGS FROM GRACE

1. Robert Murray M'Cheyne, *A Basket of Fragments* (Inverness, Scotland: Christian Focus Publications, 1979), p. 8.
2. Cleon L. Rogers Jr. and Cleon L. Rogers III, *New Linguistic & Exegetical Key to the Greek New Testament* (Grand Rapids, MI: Zondervan, 2003; Pradis Electronic Version produced by Zondervan Interactive, 2004).

CHAPTER TWENTY-FOUR: WE ARE RICH!

1. Cleon L. Rogers Jr. and Cleon L. Rogers III, *New Linguistic & Exegetical Key to the Greek New Testament* (Grand Rapids, MI: Zondervan, 2003; Pradis Electronic Version produced by Zondervan Interactive, 2004).

CHAPTER TWENTY-FIVE: THE HOPE OF GLORY

1. E. Stanley Jones, *The Word Became Flesh* (Nashville: Abingdon Press, 1963), p. 382.
2. Most of this material has been taken from Jane Stuart Smith and Betty Carlson, *Great Christian Hymn Writers* (Wheaton, IL: Crossway Books, 1997), pp. 59-64.

CHAPTER TWENTY-SIX: JESUS: OUR MESSAGE

1. Lesslie Newbigin, *The Open Secret* (Grand Rapids, MI: Eerdmans, 1978), p. 191.
2. *Spurgeon at His Best*, comp. Tom Carter (Grand Rapids, MI: Baker, 1988), p. 109.
3. Ibid., p. 110.
4. Peter Lewis, *The Glory of Christ* (London: Hodder & Stoughton, 1992), pp. 1-2 (italics his).

CHAPTER TWENTY-SEVEN: DISCIPLES ARE MADE, NOT BORN

1. William D. Mounce, editor, *Mounce's Complete Expository Dictionary of Old and New Testament Words* (Grand Rapids, MI: Zondervan, 2006), p. 793.
2. Ibid., p. 506.
3. Walter A. Henrichsen, *Disciples Are Made, Not Born* (Wheaton, IL: Victor Books, 1974).
4. Leroy Eims, *The Lost Art of Disciple Making* (Grand Rapids, MI: Zondervan, 1978).
5. John T. Seamands, *Daybreak: Daily Devotions from Acts and Pauline Epistles* (Wilmore, KY: privately published, 1993), January 17.
6. See my *Crucial Questions about Hell* (Eastbourne, UK: Kingsway, 1991; Wheaton, IL: Crossway Books, 1994; Mumbai, India: GLS, 2003), Chapters 12-13.
7. Cited in Martin E. Marty, "Hell Disappeared, No One Noticed. A Civic Argument," *Harvard Theological Review,* Vol. 78 (3-4) (1985), p. 386.

CHAPTER TWENTY-EIGHT: TIREDNESS IN DISCIPLE-MAKING

1. Kent Hughes, *The Disciplines of a Godly Man*, Tenth Anniversary Edition, Revised Edition (Wheaton, IL: Crossway Books, 2001), p. 214.
2. Barclay Newman, *New Testament Greek-English Dictionary* (Reading, UK: United Bible Societies).
3. Hughes, *Disciplines of a Godly Man*, p. 197.
4. *George Mueller: Man of Faith*, ed. A. Sims (privately published in Singapore by Warren Myers), p. 52; taken from *An Hour with George Mueller* (Grand Rapids, MI: Zondervan), p. 51.

CHAPTER TWENTY-NINE: HE GIVES THE STRENGTH

1. Robert Murray M'Cheyne, *A Basket of Fragments* (Inverness, Scotland: Christian Focus Publications), p. 6.

CHAPTER 30: A PARADOX OF THE CHRISTIAN LIFE

1. Quoted in Eberhard Bethge, *Bonhoeffer: An Illustrated Biography* (London: Found Paperbacks, HarperCollins Publishers, 1979), p. 62.
2. Dietrich Bonhoeffer, *Meditations on the Cross*, ed. Manfred Weber, trans. Douglas W. Stott (Louisville: Westminster John Knox Press, 1998), p. 9.
3. Dietrich Bonhoeffer, *The Cost of Discipleship*, Part, 1 quoted in *Meditations on the Cross,* pp. 11-12.
4. Bonhoeffer, *The Cost of Discipleship*, Part, 1 quoted in *Meditations on the Cross,* p. 12.
5. Bonhoeffer, *Meditations on the Cross,* p. 46.
6. Bethge, *Bonhoeffer: An Illustrated Biography*, p. 80.
7. Ibid., p. 84.

SCRIPTURE INDEX

Name Index